"Gil has created a masterful model of leadership in his book that contradicts the old adage that 'leaders are born and not made'. The book is an easy read that provides clarity on all the attributes to become an effective leader. Companies should use it to create leaders at all levels within their organization."

Jerome Maxwell
Managing Director, Alcoa JV Jamalco Alumina Refinery

"I have used Crosby's leadership coaching for the past two decades, and it has consistently paid off for me personally and for the organizations I have led. I strongly endorse this book for anyone in a leadership position, whether they are just starting out or are in an executive-level position and deep into their career. The guidance and insights regarding clarity about self and about how to connect with and align the organization are critically important."

Senior Utility Executive

"I loved the easy way you made the complex seem simple. Your exposition of EQ/EI in operational terms/level is the best I have read, bar none. I felt as if I had to slog thru other books on the matter. Yours was so cogent and immensely relatable. It simultaneously illuminated and clarified. I could not stop reading that section—savoring each thought! The thought kept coming to mind: 'Gil, you sure can write, me lad'."

Edward Hampton
Founder, Performance Perspectives LLC, Organizational Performance Consultant and Coach

"I am grateful for Crosby's book, which brings together critically important interpersonal behavior, vision, management, and systems strategy to promote best leadership behavior for results. In the nonprofit environment, leaders will find these concepts accessible and immediately useful."

Janis Avery
CEO, Treehouse

"Gil brings together core ideas about leading. The key is to have courage to lead while staying connected and especially staying connected with the nay-sayers! Gil provides concrete steps on how to do this!"

Behzad Suroosh
President, Starbucks Germany

"My exposure to the Crosby approach to Emotional Intelligence was not only a blessing in my workplace but also a blessing in my life! Until forces beyond our control intervened, Crosby helped management and labor at our plant come together in a remarkable and productive collaboration. I would highly recommend Gil Crosby's book and services to anyone looking to better their business success or their personal success!"

Pat Roberson
Former Union Steward, Aluminum Rolling Mill

"Success in leadership starts with an understanding of yourself, and then learning how to understand others. *Leadership Can Be Learned* takes you on a journey of integrating these two concepts and provides insights and practical contributions to help you become a more effective leader."

Carolyn A. Reid-Cater
Manager Human Resources, Walt Disney Parks & Resorts

"I first interacted with the Crosbys way back in 1997 when I attended their Tough Stuff program as a young engineer in one of Alcoa's closure manufacturing plants in the United States. Over the years, as my responsibilities grew and I faced new business challenges around the world, I regularly reached out to the Crosbys for help. Gil and his brother Chris helped me teach, practice, and instill the key principles highlighted in this book with my work teams in the United States, Egypt, and Europe. These principles have been a key contributor toward my success and growth in the business world. I highly recommend Gil's new book to anyone who wants to be an effective leader."

Sunil Sharma
Chief Strategy Officer, Midal Cables Ltd

"'The biggest variable isn't who is on the bus; the biggest variable is how the bus is being driven...' This simple-but-profound quote from Crosby captures the essence of learning to lead. In his book, you will find trustworthy sources of wisdom and competence that result in true leadership. A clear, provocative, and inspiring must-read for any leader or leader-to-be."

Dr. John J. Scherer
Director, Scherer Leadership Int., author of Five Questions
That Change Everything

"Gil Crosby's guidance has provided me clear and repeatable results in diverse situations. The improvements in team member interactions are seamlessly linked to business outcomes. Gil helps leaders make clear and direct connection with their teams, and he helps everyone be a leader. His approach improves results while strengthening the bonds within the organization. Crosby brings focus to key issues in direct and memorable ways— 'don't chase the stray cows'. Crosby's approach naturally builds trust while achieving desired results."

Tom Mitchell
CEO, Sherwin Alumina Refinery

"I had been a passionate believer in 'leaders are born, not made', before I met Gil. We have had the opportunity to engage Gil on numerous occasions to work with key leaders struggling with communication and relationship issues with their employees. I watched him repeatedly not only help fix the group but also change the thought processes and interaction skills of the leads of those groups—he converted them from managers to leaders in front of my very eyes. In *Leadership Can Be Learned*, he gives away his secrets and tactics, which I saw, firsthand, work and work very well! I am an avid student, to say the least."

Utility Executive

I met Gil when I had just started working at Jamalco in Clarendon, Jamaica. He led us on a course called Tough Stuff. I resisted the concept. I next joined Honeywell, providing services to Jamalco. This involved working with many groups. I called upon Gil to work with these groups so we can work better together, and it was then that I understood what he taught and the link to the previous Tough Stuff course that I had resisted years back. I quickly enrolled myself and a colleague to redo the course with him, Chris, his brother, and Bob, his dad. It was great. I have been a student of what Gil and his organization has taught ever since. I have read Gil's previous book and many of his dad's books, and this book is a continuation of the excellence that always comes out. I do believe that leadership can be learned, and when anyone reads it, I am confident that he or she shall agree!

Gobind Dansinghani
Quasar Site Services Manager, Jamalco Process Control Dept.

"In over 17 years of working with Gil, he has inspired me to command confidence and be an insightful visionary leader. His teachings clearly come through in this book. His interactions with clients and various teams locally and internationally have incited transformation from organizational status quo to high-performance, resulting in team cohesiveness, retention of staff, increased productivity, and generated revenue. Gil intellectually stimulates creativity and communicates on such high levels as to make good leaders into exceptional and influential ones. Furthermore, his unique ability as an organizational coach has enabled my organizations to embrace cultural variation, promote acceptance, and foster collaboration in diverse international locations including India, Jamaica, and the United States. He promotes high moral and ethical practices within companies and commands high respect. Gil's efficiency, expertise, and unique ability to develop leadership skills makes me fully endorse his authority on the topic of leadership in his writings."

Alumina Refinery Operations Director

"I've been able to engage Gil as a leadership consultant in two different manufacturing organizations, helping me and the teams I led reach new levels of performance. One was a business turnaround situation and the other a business needing drastic change to ramp up to much higher levels of productivity. The first business went from being a money loser to one of the best in its industry. The second achieved rapid increases in productivity and quality. Gil's vast experience in engaging leaders and teams enables him to meet people right where they are at and uncover what is blocking peak performance. His new book will help leaders to gain new insights as to how they can improve themselves leading to greater personal satisfaction and bottom-line business results."

Tim Howard
Retired Plant Manager

"I must confess. When asked to review your book and read the title, I had a flash of cynicism. Another how-to-lead, written by a consultant… not a leader? After reviewing, I now view your ideas as incredibly useful. Because you write from a consultant's perspective, you bring critical issues, normally hidden to leaders, into the light. I especially like your goal of "knowing yourself and understanding others in a new way." This anchors the abstraction 'leadership' into real-life, real-situation, know yourself. So it's a wonderful challenge to those who want to lead. Also, if I had the job of designing leadership training, your book would be a must."

Dr. Ron Short
Author of A Special Kind of Leadership

"Your book sounds/looks interesting AND publishable. Here's what I suggest: send a HARD COPY of the book to my home address and I'll see what I can do."

Dr. Warren Bennis
Renowned leadership expert, after reading the manuscript for Leadership Can Be Learned shortly before his death in 2014

Leadership Can Be Learned

Clarity, Connection, and Results

Leadership Can Be Learned

Clarity, Connection, and Results

Gilmore Crosby

CRC Press
Taylor & Francis Group
Boca Raton London New York

CRC Press is an imprint of the
Taylor & Francis Group, an **informa** business

A PRODUCTIVITY PRESS BOOK

CRC Press
Taylor & Francis Group
6000 Broken Sound Parkway NW, Suite 300
Boca Raton, FL 33487-2742

© 2018 by Gilmore Crosby
CRC Press is an imprint of Taylor & Francis Group, an Informa business

No claim to original U.S. Government works

Printed on acid-free paper

International Standard Book Number-13: 978-1-138-29742-5 (Hardback)
International Standard Book Number-13: 978-1-315-09929-3 (eBook)

Library of Congress Cataloging-in-Publication Data

Names: Crosby, Gilmore, author.
Title: Leadership can be learned : clarity, connection, and results / Gilmore Crosby.
Description: Boca Raton, FL : CRC Press, 2018. | Includes bibliographical references and index.
Identifiers: LCCN 2017029314| ISBN 9781138297425 (hardback : alk. paper) | ISBN 9781315099293 (ebook)
Subjects: LCSH: Leadership.
Classification: LCC HD57.7 .C7536 2018 | DDC 658.4/092--dc23
LC record available at https://lccn.loc.gov/2017029314

Visit the Taylor & Francis Web site at
http://www.taylorandfrancis.com

and the CRC Press Web site at
http://www.crcpress.com

Contents

Acknowledgments

Kurt Lewin, Murray Bowen, Edwin Friedman, Joseph Campbell, John Dewey, John Wallen, Jerome Maxwell, Tom Russell, Paul Hinnenkamp, Gobind Dansinghani, Mark Horswood, Denny Minno, Chris Crosby, Norm Myers, and first and foremost, my father and mentor, Robert P. Crosby, 89 years old at the time of this writing. Last but by no means least, I am blessed by my Jamaican rhythm and muse...my life...my wife...Alecia.

> Start with yourself. No matter how good you are, you will be caught up in some dysfunctional patterns. Whatever is not working now is being co-created by you. You are inevitably part of the dance. If you initiate change by fixing others, you'll be seen as a "do as I say, not as I do" sort of leader, cajoling others to straighten themselves out while continuing your own ineffective patterns. Don't blame the followers. Lead as a learner-leader. Quit dancing your part in the patterns you complain about. Lead with yourself. —Robert P. Crosby

Introduction

Despite all that has been written on the subject, the premise of this book is that leadership is *poorly understood* because *human systems are poorly understood*. Like the paradigms of old, which were eventually discarded—flat earth, earth at the center of the universe, and so on—most people are trapped in a limiting paradigm of personal authority and human systems. Problems are understood as "clashes of personality," and blame is directed at the superficial level of individuals, groups, and structure. The result is hardly more sophisticated than a soap opera. The true root cause is overlooked, and hence perpetuated.

There is a way out, clearly demonstrated, consistently replicated, and yet little known. This book clarifies that path, already blazed by pioneers such as Edwin Friedman and my father, organization development pioneer, Robert P. Crosby, and guides you on that path in four sections. The first section is focused on Friedman's transformational leadership model; the second, the theory of human systems from which that leadership model emerged; the third, a deep, yet practical, exploration of self-awareness and interpersonal skills related to leadership; and the fourth and final section a practical application of the aforementioned leadership model to getting results in an organization.

An equally important premise of this book is that *everybody has authority issues*. It is part of the human condition. Everybody starts life totally dependent on adults caring for them, and our beliefs, emotions, and behavioral habits regarding authority are forged in that early experience.

Despite this universal presence of authority relationships in human families and institutions, many people go through life in denial, or at least unaware, of their biases about authority. Even those teaching and writing about leadership (including me) have authority issues. Many in my profession of organization development have advocated for decades for flat organizations, "self-organizing" organizations, leaderless teams, "servant leadership," "upside-down" organizations, and a plethora of other approaches seeking a cure for the conflicts, convoluted communication, and inefficiencies that often emerge between leaders and subordinates. Tom Peters, as just one prominent example, in his bestselling *In Search of Excellence* heaped praise on the Uddevalla Volvo plant for opening its doors with leaderless teams. The same year that his book was published, sadly, the plant had to shut its doors due to low productivity/high cost production.

This is not to say that you can't make flat structures work. However, to do so, you have to have *clarity* about authority. You have to know who will decide what, how, and by when, and you need everyone as aligned as possible in support of the authority structure in your system. You also need clarity about human systems. Starting with yourself, you must lead toward a high-performance culture. Without such clarity, even in the simple structure of a hierarchy, you will have chaos.

Friedman's leadership model, in my opinion, is superior, precisely because it takes our authority issues into account, and guides each person in how to adjust and continually become a more effective and mature leader.

Leadership can be learned. Although there is art to leadership, there is also science. With this text you will gain a new understanding of human systems and of how to improve yourself and the system you are in. High-performance culture and high-performance leadership are mirror images of each other. Once you grasp the principals, the key will be in your hands.

Section I

Self-Differentiated Leadership

We begin by exploring Edwin Friedman's theory of leadership, which is the basis for both this book and the author's leadership development career.

1

Leadership

Take clear stands and stay connected—the essence of leadership. The task of being an effective authority figure remains the same, whether your role impacts many (president, vice president, CEO, etc.) or a few (parent, front line supervisor, etc.). It is, on a small yet important scale, a heroic quest that requires a true combination of art and science. This guide draws on the experiences of my father, Robert P. Crosby (who began his career in the 1950s), and I (an Organization Development Professional since 1984), along with many other sources both ancient and modern, to convey a practical and thoroughly tested model of leadership. Applied with humility and sincerity, you and the people you lead can move mountains.

The leader's quest has been undertaken since the dawn of time. The path, while illuminated by this book, is always uniquely your own. It was forged in your earliest moments, before you understood language, in the cauldron of your earliest authority relationships. You learned then about trust and mistrust, about dependency and independence. You don't need therapy to understand your current reactions to being an authority figure and to relating to authority figures (although therapy can be a path to learning). You need only to be a clear-eyed observer of your own emotional and behavioral reactions. From there, you can create your own clarity about how to be the most effective leader you can be.

To walk the path, one must balance taking clear concise stands (focusing on and trusting self) and staying connected to the people you depend on (focusing on and trusting others). Either extreme, only taking stands (leading autocratically) or only staying connected (leading by consensus), will pull you off the path. People respond to clarity and people respond to mutual respect. A transformational leader knows how to foster both. This book is about that journey. Take clear stands and stay connected and you will create your own Camelot moments of results and camaraderie.

What's so tough about taking clear stands and staying connected? As you follow your path, your own shadows will stalk you. Many who find themselves in positions of authority desire so much to be "one of the gang" or "just a regular guy" that they undermine their ability to lead. Others lose their sense of self, doing what they think is expected of them instead of what they believe to be right. Some dictate and erode the connection necessary for leading. Others are unwilling to take strong stands for fear of how people will feel.

Most, in my experience, underestimate the deep psychological importance of any formal leadership role. All humans are born completely dependent on the adult authority figures in their lives. The emotions that are experienced in those early relationships stay with us throughout life. We project them onto authority figures and live them out in our own roles of authority. To lead and/or follow effectively we must come to terms with our own reactions to authority, and we must empathize with the reactions of others. This is true whether we are a front line supervisor, a CEO, or a parent. If we let our desire "not to be the boss" keep us from taking clear stands, or if we allow our defensiveness when people react to our stands to erode the connection, then we cannot lead. To truly lead one must provide direction or the organization will flounder, and one must effectively relate or the organization will not follow.

Take clear stands and stay connected. That is the essence of Dr. Edwin Friedman's (1932–1996) model of leadership. Friedman was the protégé of family systems therapist Dr. Murray Bowen. He took Bowen's systems thinking and applied it to organizations. This book explores both the art and science of his simple yet powerful model, including how to understand yourself and develop your ability to lead and connect.

2

Vision

Vision is a great example of the blend of art and science in leadership. Clear goals and metrics must be part of vision, but they are not enough to inspire others. People want to be part of something meaningful, and the meaning must be legitimate to sustain inspiration. Sometimes meaning is handed to you from a burning platform, for example the shutdown of Peach Bottom Atomic Power Station by the NRC (a turnaround my father and I both worked on), or among the numerous manufacturing plants that face (or have already faced) extinction if they don't raise their performance to new heights, markets, etc. In other circumstances, the vision is a rebirth of a relatively successful enterprise.

Whatever the path, it is unique to your current circumstances, and must engage the hearts, minds, and discretionary efforts of your followers. It requires a clear, concise stand, and can only be accomplished through connection. You are dependent on them, and they are dependent on you. This interdependence must be embraced and respected by a critical mass of the organization (management and labor, maintenance, production, etc.). "Us versus them" is a barrier to performance. The concept of *e pluribus unum* ("out of many, one"), rooted in genuine respect for individual thought and action, is essential to performance.

To find your vision, like Arthur's knights of old, you must enter the forest on your own path. Although you must enter alone, the wise leader learns from the external environment (market conditions, changing technology, etc.) and from the people they are leading. Tapping this latter source can be one of the great opportunities for connection. Time and again I have worked with leaders who have instead made the initial mistake of "imposing their stamp on the organization" by walking in and giving significant direction before connecting and learning. One such well-intentioned leader walked in and announced he was cutting the maintenance budget by 40% (the department populated by most of the union leadership). It took him the better part of two years to overcome the reaction from the organization and create a more unified approach to pursuing efficiencies. Other leaders (several of which I have known personally) judged the culture of their organization as too passive/conflict avoidant. To correct this, they demonstrated the desired behavior: confronting like crazy. The system reacted by going into shock, and rather than adopting the desired behavior, demonized the leader as too abrasive. The masses hunkered down into even more avoidant behavior, pinning their hopes on the next change at the top (in most cases, simultaneously mythologizing their past leader, whatever their flaws might have been). As Kurt Lewin, the father of organization development, noted, push (without connection) and people push back (even while they nod their heads and say "Yes boss").

By rushing to change the culture, these leaders had to take even more time reconnecting and starting over before the organizations would allow them to lead.

Understandably, most new leaders enter with a mandate from their bosses to create change and get results as quickly as possible. But as systems theorist Edwin Friedman put it, "You can't make a bean grow by pulling on it." It's true that creating the rapport for change takes time; however, it's also true that it takes much less time than rushing, stumbling, and recovering.

Enter your new system with respect. Find out what your direct reports and cross section of the organization think is working well and what needs to be improved. This can be done in a variety of ways, including through meetings and by walking around.

Listen skillfully! Make sure you really understand their perspective. Test and demonstrate your understanding by letting them know what you think they are saying. Build your active listening skills if they don't come easily! They are critical skills for the entire organization. Anyone can state their opinion (an important ability). Understanding the opinions of others in the manner that they were really trying to convey is even more important in bringing people together to solve interdependent problems (most problems in organizations!). If you think you know what people mean, especially when you don't like what you think they mean, question your own thinking! The only way to know for sure that you got the message in the way it was intended is to verbally verify. In behavioral science terms, this is called paraphrasing (for more on this, read Appendix A). That is, you have to tell them what you think they meant, and give them a chance to say "Yes that's it," or to say "No" or "Not quite" and attempt to clarify. Otherwise, you risk parting ways thinking you have understood when it is quite possible you haven't. This is more common than most people realize, and creates a lot of needless confusion and tension in organizations. To connect effectively, you need to be a source of clarity and accuracy about your views and the views of others. As the new leader, you are an emotional lightning rod. If you are accidentally more a source of misunderstanding than understanding, then you will create chaos and fail to establish the connection you need to lead. Since connection is critical to leading, how to develop both your active listening and emotional intelligence skills are explored in great detail in this book.

Through this period of connecting, you will learn many things, as well as verify and challenge some of your own assumptions. Finally, and at least equally important, you will demonstrate that you have respect for the people you are attempting to lead. Perhaps your vision will be the same one you walked in with, perhaps it will be radically different. To succeed, your vision doesn't have to be fancy, but it does need to be clear. My father, in his book *Cultural Change in Organizations*, introduced the following model (see figure below) for, so to speak, organizing the organization.

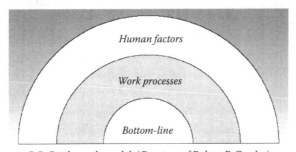

R.P. Crosby goals model. (Courtesy of Robert P. Crosby.)

As you can see, he divided the organization's goals into three categories. The bottom line is the standard focus, representing system-wide targets. Although the platform hadn't caught fire yet, one wise leader drew a simple graphic showing that his plant was the highest-cost producer of alumina in a seven-plant system. His target was to get to third lowest cost, essentially tied with two much larger plants that had the advantage of scale. He included several process targets to enable the broad target, such as reducing raw material waste and energy costs. Then he used a human factors strategy, a system-wide planning intervention designed by my father that brought a cross section of the plant together to diagnose, plan, and implement solutions to problems targeted by the vision, intact and cross-functional work team development, and the training of a cross section of the workforce in emotional intelligence and conflict management skills, to move the organization forward. They met and exceeded their targets.

PECO Nuclear, soon after the Peach Bottom shut down, targeted going from worst to first as measured by industry standards. They used many of the same human factors strategies listed in the last example. They also learned that they had to adjust their bottom line goals to clearly involve safety and quality, when some workers interpreted the production target and a culture of "making it happen" to imply that industrial safety precautions could be overlooked in the pursuit of getting things done. After a couple of near misses, the leadership team successfully righted the course to pursue high performance, but never at the expense of quality or safety. They walked that talk, including publically criticizing themselves for sending a confusing message by rewarding such "heroics" in the past, and the organization adjusted by maintaining high performance without taking risks.

So the question is not only what kind of bottom line and process goals are you after, but also what kind of culture are you trying to create. For instance, are you trying to break down silos (i.e., minimize the damaging effects of "us versus them")? Besides taking a clear stand with clarity about how breaking down silos will help you hit your bottom line and process goals, you need a human factors strategy aligned with your vision. For instance, you might take a careful look at whether your current system of departmental goals rewards one part of the organization (the warehouse, for example) for hitting its targets (low inventory/low costs) by starving other parts of the organization (making it hard for maintenance and production to get needed parts and equipment). Furthermore, you will almost certainly have to push people and groups into coming together cross-functionally if you want them to solve process and cross-group dilemmas. Left to their own devices and habits, they will be tempted to stay in their silos (and blame the rest of the organization from a "safe" distance).

To help break down silos, goal alignment should be truly systemic. To the extent possible weight your performance management system toward individual rewards based on hitting large cross-functional and systemic targets, rather than strictly or mostly on evaluation of individual performance (for more on performance management, read Chapter 9; for more on goal setting and goal alignment strategy, read Chapter 10). If you want teamwork across the system, figure out how to reward interdependence, not independence. Finally, make sure your people have the necessary skills to effectively handle cross-functional conversations (which are the same skills you need, such as active listening, in order to lead and connect).

Breaking down silos, of course, is just one example of a possible human factors goal. Whatever the goal, getting clear about your personal role in implementation is critical. One leader, with a vision of creating a culture where people would openly surface work issues, put her personal commitment this way: "At times you will be upset with my decisions or my behavior. That is inevitable. Then you will have a choice. I sincerely ask…don't hide your thoughts and feelings from me. Even if I find them difficult, I will respect you all the more for speaking them. This is the culture I vow to live, and this is the culture we must have throughout the organization to reach our highest potential."

Find your vision; take clear concise stands on it; and stay connected.

3

Vision Is Not Enough

Burnside

"Oh those men, those men over there! I cannot get them out of my mind" (Fair, 1971). Such was the lament of General Ambrose E. Burnside (pictured above), after he sent 12,653 men to be killed or wounded charging unprotected up a hill into withering fire from General Robert E. Lee's Confederate army at Fredericksburg, Virginia. Burnside never wavered from his vision, despite the pleadings of capable subordinates, who could see with perfect clarity that attacking Lee's men, who were behind a stone wall at the top of a hill, was folly. He ordered the attack and then sat back in his headquarters awaiting the execution of his commands. It was strategy (bordering on wishful thinking) without tactics. As if to punctuate this point, when the

Union army punched a hole in the Confederate line through some woods to the left of the hill, Burnside chose not to send reinforcements. Instead he allowed this promising attack to falter, and rigidly stuck to his doomed vision of taking the hill. Interestingly, despite this and other infamous disasters (he may have singlehandedly lost the battle of Antietam, among other things), Burnside remained a popular leader, having been twice elected to the US Senate from Rhode Island. And the word "sideburns" literally traces back to this man and his bold style of facial hair.

History is full of contrasts between leaders who set direction and then make adjustments, and those who are too detached to know what is really going on. Two leaders, Napoleon Bonaparte (photo below) and Robert E. Lee, made this contrast evident by succeeding when they made adjustments and failing when they did not.

Napoleon

In his prime, Napoleon was a master of battlefield tactics, such as marching secretly behind the Austrian army, striking their flank, and defeating them soundly at Ulm, Germany. While his subordinates capably executed his tactical decisions, he was clearly the master of the situation, keeping a close eye on the ever changing conditions and adjusting his plans accordingly.

We can only speculate why (illness and fatigue may have played a role… imagine traveling by horse or even coach from Paris to Moscow!) but in key battles late in his career, notably at Borodino and Waterloo, Napoleon hung back, leaving the execution of his plan and tactical adjustments in the hands of his immediate subordinates. Unfortunately for him, they weren't up to the task. Their blunders were many, culminating with Field Marshall Ney's ill-advised decision to send the entire French cavalry, 12,000 men, into an unsupported charge against the center of the Duke of Wellington's line at Waterloo. Napoleon's normal discipline of coordinating his artillery, infantry, and cavalry attacks was neglected in the heat of the moment, and the gallant French cavalry was cut down along with any hope of victory. Wellington, in contrast, took a hands-on approach, writing later that it "was the nearest run thing you ever saw in your life" also noting that "I was always on the spot—I saw everything, and did everything myself" (Garnet, 1976). This of course is not literal (his army did its fair share) but Wellington was indeed orchestrating the necessary adjustments of his forces himself, sending his reserves at the last moment to the very point of the French cavalry attack. Without his active leadership, the battle would almost certainly have been lost.

Robert E. Lee's tale is similar to Napoleon's, although not due to over-relying on his subordinates, but rather to abandoning his own past practice at a critical moment that turned the course of the Civil War. As mentioned, at Fredericksburg, Lee (photo on next page) chose a strong defensive position (the top of a hill, behind a wall), and then was rewarded as Burnside sent the Union army forward like lambs to the slaughter. Following Burnside's dismissal by Lincoln, Lee again outwitted his replacement, General "Fighting Joe" Hooker, at the battle of Chancellorsville, this time with audacious offensive tactics.

Hooker's strategy was reasonable enough. Move a sizeable force upstream and strike the confederates, still entrenched at Fredericksburg, in the rear. Unfortunately for Fighting Joe, Lee anticipated this move, and made his own bold counter move, splitting his forces and sending Stonewall Jackson around Hooker's rear where he launched an attack at nightfall that sent the Union forces into a panic. As Lee attacked from one side and Jackson from the other, Hooker became first indecisive, and then was literally knocked senseless when a cannonball shattered a post he was leaning on. The only decisive action he took was to stubbornly refuse to relinquish command, even as he simultaneously failed to give desperately needed direction. The battle became a route, with the Union losing 4,139 more men than they had in the folly at Fredericksburg. The South paid dearly though when Jackson, a brilliant tactician, was accidentally cut down by his own men in the falling darkness, the occupational hazard of leading in the front.

Lee

Lee's quick tactical adjustment, from a strong defensive position to hitting the enemy with surprise and in their weakest point, paid off at Chancellorsville, as his tactics often did throughout the war. At the battle of Gettysburg, rather than outwitting his opponent, Lee tried to overpower them, launching a frontal assault on a heavily-defended position. The cream of his army marched across open fields and up a hill into the teeth of Union artillery and rifle fire (as at Fredericksburg, entrenched behind a stone wall) in the now infamous "Pickett's Charge" (photo below). Only 250 or so reached the goal, and were easily overwhelmed by the defenders. Half of Pickett's 15,000 men died in the assault. The remainder retreated in defeat.

Pickett's Charge

The Confederacy never again mounted a serious offensive into the North, and the war became an inevitable battle of bloody attrition, as the Union essentially wore down the South with superior numbers.

Uncharacteristically, Lee had abandoned his clever tactics in favor of a reckless charge into an excellent defensive position. As with Napoleon's shift to a "hands-off" approach, *why* will forever be a mystery, but it's a clear and tragic example of when "vision is not enough."

In sum, Burnside stuck rigidly to his vision, ignoring the pleas of his subordinates that could have averted disaster. Napoleon was a superb tactician when he was hands-on, but failed to instill the same tactical discipline in his subordinates, leading to disaster when they were abruptly required to think on their own. Hooker's vision was better than his ability to adjust, and when he needed to delegate authority he failed to do so. Finally, Lee abandoned past practices of patient tactics to gamble on a "quick fix" that was almost certainly doomed to fail.

While there are many lessons to be learned from these stories, the emphasis here is that *strategy rarely unfolds the way one envisions it. A wise leader stays abreast of conditions in the field by actively listening to people at all levels of the organization, and then helps the organization adjust.* In contrast, some leaders are out of touch with their subordinates and others seem so determined to work through them that they lose touch with the situations and the people below. In the latter case, some worry (due to past experience) that if they "think out loud" employees will take the conversation as an order, resulting in wasted activity and confusion about the chain of command. *Prevent that by being as clear as you can* ("I'm just thinking out loud...I'm not asking you to do anything!") *not by restricting your interactions.* Furthermore, at every level, one must work to prevent misunderstanding by sharpening the quality of conversations. Don't settle for generalizations such as "It's going well" or "This place is falling apart." Inquire *what specifically* is working, and *what specifically* isn't working. *Clarify your intentions with your direct reports as well.* Staying in touch below them doesn't mean that you don't trust them, that you want to undermine their authority, or that you aren't going to rely on them for information and advice. It does mean that you don't want to *over*-rely on them for information because you want to prevent their blind spots from becoming your own. No matter how well intentioned, it is easy for people to be too attached to their own positions and departments and miss the way in which their own groups are contributing to problems. Your job is to help ensure all think across the entire system.

To lead you must stay connected with a critical mass, one way or another. Too much distance erodes one's ability to rally people to action. Staying connected is both an art and a science. Don't take over decision-making authority that belongs below you, but do keep in direct contact with as much of the organization as you can. Incorporate what you see and hear into strategy and tactics at your own level. If you are implementing Lean manufacturing, for example, and your organization has over-adjusted by starving the plant of spare parts, do what it takes to get the right amount of spare parts! If you have *de-centralized any function* such as engineering (by moving the engineers into the field), keep an eye on whether plant-wide projects are now being neglected. Conversely, if you have *centralized* a function such as engineering so that they can concentrate on systemic improvements, make sure there are still engineering resources available for problem-solving emergent production issues. *No vision is perfect without adjustments!* Set your strategy, stay connected, and be prepared to adjust.

Section II

Self-Differentiated Leadership and Systems

Leadership cannot exist in a vacuum. Section 2 begins by further exploring Dr. Edwin Friedman's theory of leadership and then moves on into Bowen and Friedman's version of systems thinking. The systems you are in provide the challenges and the context for leading, including the constant tension between leading and connecting.

4

Leadership and Systems Thinking

A colleague in the nuclear industry once asked my opinion of the role "boss stress" plays in what is known in that industry as "nuclear safety culture." Research (study after study indicates that the boss–subordinate relationship is the biggest variable in job satisfaction, turnover, etc.), experience, and common sense all indicate that authority relationships are one of if not *the* biggest variable in any human system. Yet authority dynamics are poorly understood, and almost randomly executed. An excellent and practical model of the systemic impact of authority relations is the five behavioral characteristics of "chronically anxious systems" detailed by systems thinking pioneer Edwin Friedman. Additionally, based on my experiences working in industrial settings, I have added a sixth characteristic, "Error Likely," that I'm confident adheres to Friedman's logic. Friedman noted the following predictable behavioral symptoms in any organization where the leaders are more a source of unnecessary stress than they are a source of calm, focused effort. Each and all result in poor performance:

Reactivity—People go into fight and flight reactions such as keeping their mouth shut, talking behind people's backs, forming and holding negative judgments and believing them to be objective, etc. (My first book, *Fight, Flight, Freeze*, takes a detailed look at the behavioral implications of the reactive or reptilian/primitive brain.) The result is unresolved, needless drama, an overabundance of career-damaging negative evaluations, and high turnover.

Herding—People over-identify with their own groups (us vs. them) and are more concerned about their rights than their responsibilities. The focus is on "How can they treat me/us this way?", "They just don't understand," and "If they were different everything would be fine around here." The results are poor alignment, miscommunication, and defensiveness. These behaviors, along with the following characteristics, kill the upward and lateral communication essential to safety and high performance.

Displaced blame—People point in every other direction rather than calmly looking at their own role in what has gone wrong and what could make it better. Feedback, when it happens, tends to be negative and is likely to be defensively ignored.

Quick fix mentality—This is an epidemic. Symptoms include trying to implement too many solutions at the same time, poor implementation, and always looking for the next best thing because past efforts have failed to produce the intended results. Friedman's metaphor, "You can't make a bean grow by pulling on it," is worth repeating here. Many sound solutions get bungled because of quick fix thinking. The root cause (i.e., the "quick fix mentality") tends to be overlooked and is defended as a "sense of urgency" (all the more confusing because "a sense of urgency" is appropriate and much needed in many systems). Therefore, the people and failed solutions tend to be blamed instead.

Error likely—People in a chronically anxious system are more likely to make mistakes leading to quality, safety, and other consequences. Programmatic approaches to safety will be inhibited by the previously listed characteristics. In a worst case scenario, safety programs may actually become a source of additional performance-eroding stress.

Absence of nonanxious leadership—This is the ultimate root cause of all of the above and it replicates itself in a dysfunctional system.

To use another Friedman metaphor, an anxious leader is like a "step-up transformer" in the organization's emotional system. At precisely the time the organization needs clear calm leadership and predictable behavior from their leader(s), the leader's own anxiety spikes and increases the emotional intensity in the system, thus at best becoming something to "cope with" and at worst becoming an actual deterrent to performance. In contrast, Friedman advocates for an emotionally intelligent approach (although he didn't use that term). To be a self-differentiated leader you must function the majority of the time as a "step-down transformer," helping the emotional system stay cool, calm, and focused during difficult moments, *even if you yourself are anxious and uncertain of the outcome.*

Allow me to further illustrate Friedman's model of non-anxious leadership by comparing the shared traits of two of my heroes, General George

S. Patton and Mahatma Gandhi. Both leaders embodied the second characteristic of self-differentiated leadership, as defined by Friedman, *the capacity and the willingness of the leader to take nonreactive, clearly conceived, and clearly defined positions.*

When you take a clear stand, you will almost certainly face conflict from one quarter or the other. Better men than I, such as Patton and Gandhi (Figures 4.1 and 4.2), certainly did. But those who try to avoid conflict by

FIGURE 4.1
Mahatma Gandhi. (From Shutterstock, Stock illustration ID: 554720683—Gandhi. With permission.)

FIGURE 4.2
General George S. Patton Jr. (re-enactor). (From Shutterstock, Stock illustration ID: 106137374—Patton. With permission.)

avoiding clarity, or by agreeing with everyone, are doomed to mediocrity. They cannot lead. "Followers" cannot channel their energy without clarity about where they are heading. As my father puts it (paraphrasing both John Dewey and Kurt Lewin), "There is no freedom without structure." Clear direction adds essential structure to human systems.

Gandhi took a clear stand on nonviolence, and many of his peers thought he was crazy. Patton always looked to break through a small point and go around the enemy, while most of his peers (Generals Bradley, Hodges, Eisenhower, and Montgomery, for example) believed in building up an overwhelming force and attacking across a broad front. When the allies were stuck soon after the Normandy invasion, Patton advocated openly to his superiors and lamented privately in his diary,

> They try to push all along the front and have no power anywhere. All that is necessary now is to take chances by leading men with armored divisions and covering their advance with air bursts. Such an attack would have to be made on a narrow sector where as at present we are trying to attack all along the line. (Hanson 1999)

Soon after (although not soon enough for the soldiers who died during the initial futile strategy), Patton was put in charge of the Third Army and implemented his plan, breaking through the German lines. Many of Patton's peers thought he was reckless, but ironically his methods led to far lower casualties and far greater gains.

Both Patton and Gandhi's followers knew exactly where they stood on key defining issues, and were able to execute based on that knowledge. Gandhi's position was firm and consistent (Herman 2008): "An eye for an eye makes the whole world blind." "I object to violence because when it appears to do good, the good is only temporary; the evil it does is permanent." "I cannot teach you violence, as I do not myself believe in it. I can only teach you not to bow your heads before anyone even at the cost of your life." On the occasions where his followers deviated, the consequences were terrible. Often enough, his message and methods were so clear that in an age without the mass-media technologies we take for granted today, he was able to align an entire nation in collective action. General Patton, in his own colorful language, was equally clear:

> There's another thing I want you to remember. Forget this goddamn business of worrying about our flanks...Some goddamned fool once said that flanks must be secured and since then sons of bitches all over the world

have been going crazy guarding their flanks. We don't want any of that in the Third Army. Flanks are something for the enemy to worry about, not us. I don't want to get any messages saying that, 'We are holding our position.' We're not holding anything! Let the Hun do that. We are advancing constantly and we are not interested in holding on to anything except the enemy. We're going to hold on to him by the nose and we're going to kick him in the ass; we're going to kick the hell out of him all the time and we're going to go through him like crap through a goose...We have one motto, "L'audace, l'audace, toujours l'audace!" ("Audacity, audacity, always audacity!"). Remember that gentlemen. (Herman 2008)

If you were under General Patton, you knew you were moving forward. Not foolishly, like the mass frontal attacks of WW1, but by persistently bypassing enemy strongholds thus forcing them into a position of weakness and withdrawal.

Friedman's "first and foremost characteristic" of a self-differentiated leader is equally vital: "The leader must stay in touch." As another self-differentiated leader, General William Tecumseh Sherman, put it: "no man can properly command an army from the rear" (Hanson 1999). General Stonewall Jackson, on the other side in the same conflict, wielded the same belief to great effect, often placing himself in harm's way as he reconnoitered and led the action (eventually, as mentioned in Chapter 3, resulting in his death at the Battle of Chancellorsville). The modern belief that "empowerment" and "systems" can create reliable results allowing a leader to sit in their office or attend meetings all day is a false hope. To lead, one must fight the shackles of their computer and the meeting room and get out on the floor. To lead, you must engage and learn. When you lose touch, you stop leading.

Being in touch is critical to the spirit of the organization. Not only does it give you firsthand knowledge, but it also provides employees much needed access to the leadership and faith that those in charge have some idea about what is *really* going on. Patton and Gandhi were masters of staying in touch. As historian Victor Hanson put it:

Several eyewitnesses have written that Patton came close to death several times in World War Two—targeted by German artillery, airplanes, tanks, small arms fire, and machine guns while in the air, on foot, and in a jeep. He often, like his spiritual predecessors, deliberately exposed himself to hostile fire to create elan among his troops—and to reassure himself that he had not lost his nerve...Patton was not always on the front—what commander of a quarter million men could be?—but his frequent trips there in the heat of battle reassured his commanders and gave himself a constant firsthand feel for the fighting that usually resulted in yet more emphasis on speed and advance. (Hanson 1999)

Many in positions of leadership struggle to meet this characteristic. Some are concerned that they will disempower the layers of management below them if they "skip layers." Indeed, empowering middle management and frontline supervision is well worth your attention. But it doesn't happen through absence. It happens through clear goals and behavioral expectations (such as expecting everyone to constantly be clarifying who will decide what, and by when, and by expecting everyone to surface issues and create an open flow of communication), through hands-on reinforcement of those expectations, and by staying in touch without assuming authority that belongs at another level. It is leaders that "take over" that disempower, not leaders that stay in touch.

Your presence means more to your subordinates than you are likely to realize. The impact is emotional, not rational, and vital to morale (which is an emotional phenomenon). Absent "leadership" consistently kills morale. The "rational" benefit is to hear from people in varying positions, and to be heard by them. You will earn respect just by having the guts and wisdom to get out and talk to people. If you are skilled enough at active listening that they walk away trusting that you understood their message (because you know how to verify your understanding through the vital skill of "paraphrasing," mentioned in Chapter 2 and elaborated on in Appendix A), you will both gain knowledge of your organization and even more respect. Each contact will have a ripple effect, spreading from peer to peer.

Gossip either works for you or against you. Small moments where people get to know you and feel respected will pay off big time when it is time to lead in a new or challenging direction. You can't create that connection artificially when you realize you need it. You have to build it over time.

It is equally important to not get caught in the trap of listening to different parts of the system complain about and blame others. Such behavior kills cross-functional productivity and undermines morale. The problem is, people are used to it (it happens in families), and bosses join in more often than not. Instead, if it is an important work relationship between individuals or groups, you must insist on improvement. Point them toward the others, tell them to talk, ask if they want help, and if they do not, insist that they let you know about how it went. Ask for specifics. What work process commitments are they making to each other? Who will provide what by when? That is the root cause that must be ferreted out for the sake of productivity, while simultaneously being the root cause of most cross-functional conflict. If people are getting what they need from each other, harmony is more likely than conflict.

In the name of productivity and morale, if you don't hear back from them, follow up! You must lead *and* manage (much more on this in Section IV). If they don't get it that you are serious about them improving the situation, many will let it slide. If they aren't able to improve it, they may need professional conflict-resolution help. Don't let conflict that is interfering with work simmer unresolved.

Insist that others, at all levels, do the same. Insist that they *stay in touch*, and that they insist that there is constant improvement of cross-functional work.

In other words, "walk the talk." Or, to repeat Gandhi's famous quote, "Be the change you want to see in the world" (Herman 2008). Clarify your expectations, and then live them through your interactions with the organization. Encourage your subordinates to do the same, and ask them to alert you if you seem to be unintentionally contradicting your own expectations. Encourage surfacing issues, even if, and especially if, they have "issues" with your positions or behavior. Learn to reinforce the behavior of speaking up without limiting yourself to either rejecting or acquiescing passively to what is said. *Make sure you understand.* If you manage to truly understand what people are telling you, you'll be in the best position to decide what to do.

That brings us to Friedman's third and final characteristic of self-differentiated leadership: "The Capacity to Deal with Resistance." Resistance is an element of human systems. Friedman goes so far as to say that if you are not getting resistance, you probably aren't leading. In families, the members predictably focus their attention on the "black sheep" of the system. In organizations, and each work group, it is easy to do the same. This is the "Chasing the Stray Cow" syndrome (more on this in the next chapter). When leaders get hooked on trying to convert or manage the most difficult members of their system, they actually reinforce the status of and tension with that member. Energy is drained from all. The likelihood of an impasse or ugly divorce is far higher than the likelihood of converting the resistance into true support. Yet most leaders get hooked like a moth to a flame.

Like Patton and Gandhi, the path forward is to walk the talk of the first two characteristics: be clear about what you stand for, stay in touch with all parties, and move forward. This may not break the resistance, but it won't allow resistance to bog you down.

This is not to say that the sources of resistance are "the problem." Some people are simply inclined to be the vocal minority, brave enough to be overt in their discontent. Search their comments for solvable problems, and let them help you solve them! Others, of course, will wholeheartedly follow you. The majority will probably "wait and see." Insist that everyone surfaces issues and tackles barriers! Create opportunities and structure for engagement! The real problem is not resistance. The real problem is if you fuel resistance by becoming obsessed with it.

In sum, there is such a thing as good stress and bad stress. Good stress drives us to perform. Too much stress drives performance downward. Solving problems, making improvements, delivering safely, on time, and with high quality is challenging enough. Leadership is the biggest variable in keeping the right focus, or in adding needless drama and thus fueling the six characteristics. As Friedman puts it, leaders are either a step-up transformer of bad stress or they act as a step-down transformer, thus decreasing drama and helping the organization stay calmly and persistently focused on the task at hand.

Take clear stands, stay connected, and decrease needless drama: these are the essential EQ skills of self-differentiated leadership. Foster self-differentiated leadership throughout your system and watch performance improve exponentially.

Modern jargon about leadership, such as "coaching" and "servant leadership," evokes images of a kindly leader including their people in "consensus" decision making and providing friendly support to them as they get things done. An even more radical notion, supported by the new science of chaos theory, is to eliminate positional leadership altogether, replacing it with leaderless or self-managing teams. Images such as General George S. Patton Jr. growling as he leads his troops against the Nazis hardly seem relevant in the new kinder, gentler paradigm. But General Patton, or the equally tough Mahatma Gandhi, had exactly the traits needed to lead people today, and since the dawn of time.

Patton and Gandhi in the same breath? Absolutely. Both were self-differentiated leaders, in the full spirit of Murray Bowen and Edwin Friedman's theory of leadership. Both trusted their inner guidance systems (more on this in Chapter 8), and took clearly defined stands, which at times frightened and angered people who were allegedly on "their side," such as Patton's superiors and Gandhi's "middle-class" countrymen. In a military dominated by men who thought one should wait until they had vast numerical superiority before attacking, Patton stayed firm with the belief that "dig in and you are dead" (Hanson 1999). He repeatedly raced around the defending Nazis, and arguably could have ended the war months earlier, with great savings in lives, if he hadn't been stopped time and again by his own superiors. Gandhi was so committed to the path of independence for India that he placed his life on the line, through fasts and other actions, with no assurance that he would succeed. Both were crystal clear about their goals, and led toward them relentlessly. Neither waited for consensus before acting.

That's the paradox of self-differentiated leadership: *By leading you empower.* Chaos is fine in organic systems, such as a collection of cells, but not in human affairs. To paraphrase Dad, Dewey, and Lewin, "without leadership, there is no structure, and without structure, there is no empowerment." Take clear stands, stay connected.

5

Don't Chase the Stray Cow

"That's just like my cows." I'll never forget Norm, a down-to-earth engineer who had been dealing with and managing people for decades, speaking up during the management retreat I was facilitating. I had just drawn a bell-shaped curve on a flipchart to illustrate one of Edwin Friedman's lessons on self-differentiated leadership and systems thinking (similar to Figure 5.1).

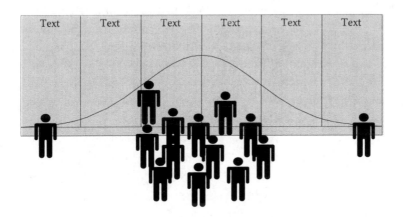

FIGURE 5.1
Self-differentiated leadership bell curve/stray cow. (Drawn by the author using Visio.)

The lesson is simple, but profound. In the vast majority of work groups, there will be some individuals who are easy for you to relate to, many who are in the middle, and one or more who drive you crazy. If the leader is thinking "nonsystemically" (as most do), the temptation is to focus a disproportionate amount of time and energy on the "problem" person. This happens in families, and since family patterns are replicated at work, the possibility is there in all work groups. Since we are creatures of habit, most leaders fall into the trap of trying to "fix" the person who becomes, in the language of family systems, "the identified patient." The problem is, it's the very pattern of focusing on that person (or persons) that pushes them further away and polarizes the organization around them.

Here again the wisdom of Kurt Lewin, the founding father of organization development, parallels that of family systems theory. Lewin was a true interdisciplinary thinker, and among other innovations, he applied physics to understanding human behavior. In Lewin's model, every driving force is met in equilibrium by restraining forces. As mentioned before, but well worth repeating, if you push, people push back. The act of resistance is fueled by the attempt to influence the identified patient, no matter how well intentioned or how logical the attempt may be. In Friedman's words, "You can't reason a man out of something he wasn't reasoned into."

Yet most leaders drag themselves down into a fruitless contest of logic and will. "If I could just convince ____, fix, or get rid of them, then things would go smooth around here." This is a trap, or as Friedman puts it, emotional sabotage. It is the very act of focusing on the identified patient that gives them their power in the system, and diminishes the leader. In meeting after meeting the leader says "Any questions?" and then turn their attention to the identified patient like iron filings to a magnet, while others passively watch, thinking, "Here we go again." Conversations with superiors, peers, and possibly even family come back time and again to "What can I/we do about ____?" The longer the pattern persists, the more the people on the fence are turned off to the entire reoccurring drama. Although they may share some of the leader's reaction to the identified patient, they also have some empathy for a peer who obviously is in disfavor, and some will get sick and tired of the "bullying" by the boss. The system is stuck. Eventually the leader and/or possibly the identified patient will go, but the pattern will almost certainly reemerge.

It's a systems issue, and it requires a systemic solution. Paradoxically, all systemic solutions start with individual awareness and behavior. That's what this book is about: how to understand yourself using an interdisciplinary approach, and how to apply that knowledge to leadership. Leaders and systems that have consistently applied these principles, the most famous being PECO Nuclear after the Peach Bottom Atomic Power Station (PBAPS) was shut down by the Nuclear Regulatory Commission (or NRC) in the late 1980s, have consistently become peak performers. You can do the same.

Consider again our group, with its leader and identified patient. To move forward, the leader must be clear about where they are heading, and then give each group member the time and respect they are due. In order to break the pattern, the leader will have to consistently speak with others. When the identified patient pipes in, the leader should make sure they understand the message, clarify any actions that they are going to take, and then move on to exploring current conditions with other group members. They should eliminate wasted time by not trying to win the identified patient over. They should also not go to the other extreme of ignoring them. They need each person, and would be wise to relate with each proportionately. If they genuinely do so, they will strengthen their bond with the majority. If they strengthen their bond with the majority, and move forward toward their goals, the identified patient will have less power in the system, and may possibly even follow their peers in following you.

Don't hold your breath on that last one, though! If that remains the leader's goal, they are still worrying about the wrong thing! What's important is the health of the overall system and to move the system forward toward the goals. To do so, a leader must recognize that they actually create resistance by getting sucked into it. The identified patient is just a symptom of dysfunctional behavior on the part of the leader! The only way out for the leader is to recognize the pattern and change their own behavior.

That is the beauty of systems thinking—the power is in our own hands more than we have been led to believe by the traditional thinking of our times and culture. You don't have to change them. You have to change yourself. Again, as Gandhi said, "Be the change you want to see in the world."

"That's just like my cows," said Norm. "When I bring them back in from pasture in the evening, one always wanders off. If I chase it, the entire herd scatters! However, if I stick with the herd, the stray cow always returns."

Humans aren't cows, but we are mammals, and relationships are vital to our development and to our behavior in organizations. Leadership requires an understanding of how emotionally connected we really are. This book will examine other patterns of human systems, like the one above, and how to lead in them. But first you must understand your own development. In the famous words of George Santayana, "Those who cannot remember the past are condemned to repeat it" (Santayana, 1905). This is as true for individuals as it is for societies. Unfortunately, critical development occurs during the first two years of life while we are precognitive. There is no way to remember it, because the capacity for cognitive memory didn't exist during the formative events. But we can "remember the past" by seeing the pattern of behavior in the present. And by seeing them, we can consciously become more stable and impactful leaders. Chapter 7 explores how we become our current selves, and how to continue becoming who we want to be. Without that type of self-knowledge, and the humility that comes with it, one is in no position to lead. Meanwhile, it is time to dig even deeper into systems thinking.

6

Systems Thinking

We are all a product of our time. Innocent in our youth, we soak up the beliefs of our culture like a sponge, quickly allowing them to harden into the filters through which we perceive and understand the world. Like the flat earth theory of old, certain beliefs or paradigms are so engrained that their wisdom and validity are taken for granted. Yet today's dominant belief about human behavior—that we have essentially fixed personalities that are the cause, at work at least, of most problems and conflicts—is as limited as the ancient belief that the world was flat. New information is available, but culturally accepted paradigms are stubborn things, slow to give way. Even when one values a new belief, when push comes to shove, it's easy to slip back into old habits. Nonetheless, a new and richer paradigm is emerging.

To fully appreciate this, the reader needs exposure to some underlying assumptions about human behavior. This chapter explores three paradigms, interlinked but distinct, offering very different possibilities for understanding and influencing human behavior.

PERSONALITY THEORY

Based loosely on psychoanalytic theory, this is the dominant paradigm in Western civilization today. Without realizing what they are doing, most people habitually rely on personality theory for understanding conflict and performance issues in organizations. Problem analysis comes to predictable conclusions such as individuals "don't have the right personality" ("he's too passive," "she micromanages," etc.) or that the root cause is a "personality clash." These sorts of personality flaws are considered essentially fixed traits. Trapped within the box of this thinking, organizations attempt to "solve" issues by moving people around and changing them out.

Ironically, the paradigm of personality theory has systemic effects (see Systems Thinking, which is the emerging alternative, below), subtly stoking the flames of organization tension. People put energy, for good reason, into worrying about how they are perceived. They know even if they are flying high today, they can be essentially written off as flawed tomorrow. That's always a possibility when organizational problems are narrowed down to individual performance. People become masters at not seeming defensive, and playing the games of feedback and development not so much for the sake of developing, but to avoid being labeled as deficient. It is a paradigm afflicted by tunnel vision ("They're having a personality clash") that is in its essence insulting to the individual, thus eliciting defensiveness and brewing CYA behavior.

Despite its flaws, personality theory is a practical paradigm that helps us understand ourselves and others. We certainly bring our individual strengths and weaknesses to the organization, and are wise to take an active approach to our own development. We are responsible for our own behavior and performance. But there are stronger forces at play than our personality traits, and to focus primarily on personality is like sticking entirely to snail mail in the age of the computer.

The computer age, incidentally, has contributed heavily to the emerging paradigm. But first, another prevalent paradigm that has its place, but only completes some of the human performance puzzle.

BEHAVIORAL THEORY

By this we mean the aspect of behavioral theory that focuses on skills. In other words, the solution to conflict and performance issues lies in a skills gap, which could be technical or interpersonal, or both. This paradigm has led to the dramatic growth of training and development as a strategy for improving organization performance. Like personality theory, it's a paradigm that makes sense to many (as it must, to become a paradigm) and has practical applications, but again overlooks powerful influences impacting individual and organizational performance.

By all means, a critical mass of individuals who, through training, have worked on their own emotional intelligence, honed their conflict management skills, studied their personality tendencies through tools such as the Meyers–Briggs Type Indicator, and learned to respect and stretch into new behaviors can move an organization to higher productivity. But as most people know, there are mysterious forces at play that can derail even the best classroom learning, especially if the paradigm underlying the training is blind to those forces.

SYSTEMS THINKING

Many have heard of it, few have made it a way of life. Rooted in computer science (Forrester), social science (Lewin), and family systems therapy (Bowen), this is arguably the most powerful element of productivity and conflict, yet it is a relatively new paradigm that is not yet integrated into popular consciousness. Some core concepts of systems thinking include the following.

START WITH YOURSELF

Most people put their time and energy into analyzing and trying to change everyone else (a by-product of the personality theory paradigm). The predictable result is defensiveness by others. If one is not skillful at analyzing oneself and working on continuous improvement (which is greatly enhanced by earnestly and skillfully soliciting feedback from others, a skillset covered in Chapter 13), then one is not likely to be a significant influence on others (although positional authority may lead others to half-hearted compliance).

OVERFUNCTIONING VS. UNDERFUNCTIONING

Everyone overfunctions or underfunctions to some degree. If I'm vocal, for example, others are likely to be less vocal. It's physics applied to human interaction. Even if I wish others were more vocal with me, my filling of airtime decreases their need/opportunity to do so. And, vice versa, if I don't speak much, others will speak more. The only way to change such a dance is to change my own behavior (in this example, speak more or speak less). The key is to be aware of such patterns and to be intentional about changing them.

Now think about your role in the organization (not necessarily your formal role, but no doubt related to it). Whatever you worry about/do that no one else seems to be worrying about/doing as much as you think they should, you are probably overfunctioning, which is likely a large reason they are underfunctioning. Classic examples are safety, quality, and HR (in terms of employee morale). These functions are far more effective when there is balance in the system, i.e., everyone is worrying about their own safety, process quality, and each supervisor is accountable for the morale of their own team (which study after study shows is largely based on their relationship with their direct reports). In a balanced system, the line organization is leading layer by layer through safety pre-job assessments and the like. If there is balanced responsibility, then the line will see safety, quality, and morale as their responsibility and will be pulling on the specialists in the system to assist them. If there is imbalance, then the specialists will be viewed more like cops, and the rest of the system will resist them. The desired performance will be far more difficult to obtain.

Whatever the symptoms in a system (accidents, etc.), overfunctioning and underfunctioning may be playing a role. If your direct reports seem incapable of doing some of the tasks they should be doing, you may be enabling their behavior by doing too much of it for them. Start with yourself. Stop blaming (which is a symptom of overfunctioning and underfunctioning), and start a dialogue about how to appropriately shift the responsibility. Plan and monitor the transition, but know this: like a parent teaching a child to ride a bike, at some point you will have to let go for them to come up to speed.

EVERY PART OF THE SYSTEM IS A REFLECTION OF THE WHOLE

Morale and productivity are not, for the most part, a personality issue. Multiple studies (including one conducted by my father, involving over 500 organizations) have linked variables such as feeling respected by one's boss, being able to influence one's work processes, and being able to make decisions at the lowest possible level, to morale and productivity. While there will always be a few who are demoralized in a system where most are productive and in high spirits, the vast majority is responsive, for better or worse, to systemic conditions. And each individual in the system, each work group, each meeting is a window into understanding the system. Whatever part of a system is struggling the most, it is somehow a reflection of the weaknesses inherent in the larger system. If the front line supervisors are perceived to be "the problem" (a common perception), then they are likely not being supervised effectively, and so on up the food chain, or in some other way being set up for failure (too large a span of control, etc.). Only a systemic approach will truly solve systemic issues.

THE LEADER IS THE BIGGEST VARIABLE IN A HUMAN SYSTEM

The emotional intelligence work of Daniel Goleman, while primarily a personality and skills approach, has helped increase awareness of systems thinking by emphasizing the amplified impact that the leader has on the emotional health of the system. The leader is not, of course, the only variable. A systemic approach encourages everyone to start with themselves, and fosters ownership and involvement at every level. Nonetheless, the emotional and systemic intelligence of the hierarchical leadership remains the biggest variable. With this in mind, Chapter 8 provides self-development guidance on emotional intelligence.

THE EMOTIONAL FIELD

People are more connected than they realize. Your emotion affects others (are you tense or relaxed?). Your approach to the conversation affects others (are you putting all of your energy into being heard, or are you also listening?). Your past impacts you and hence others (your history with a person or a group, how you feel about positional authority, etc.). The same can be said of everyone.

Family systems therapists call this convergence of past and present variables the "emotional field." Like gravity, it's invisible. You can only tell it is there by the effects. If it is a strong field, the effects are predictable. For example, if a boss is (or seems) displeased with us, most people react just as they did as a child when disciplined by their parents. They get sucked into the field of parent–child emotionality. We become more practiced at hiding our reactions, but the internal experience is much the same.

TRIANGULATION

Triangulation is yet another pattern identified in the family systems theory of Bowen and Friedman. Triangulation warrants extra attention here. Indeed, Friedman, in his book on leadership entitled *A Failure of Nerve*, writes, "… the concept of an emotional triangle is so basic to understanding relationship process and the process of a leader's self-differentiation that this entire book could have been cast in its terms." It is a pattern common to all human cultures, and it is equally prevalent at home and at work. As with any behavioral pattern, freedom to choose your own behavior begins with awareness. If you can't recognize a pattern, you're doomed to repeat it.

Triangulation occurs when two (or more) parties commiserate together about a third party (or topic), rather than working on their issues directly with the third party. It is a dysfunctional yet common approach to coping with conflict. Therefore, before continuing our discussion of triangulation, it's important to return to the presence of personality theory in modern culture when it comes to conflict.

Culture, simply put, is a mix of the dominant behaviors and beliefs prevalent in a society, family, or organization. Without realizing the roots of their beliefs, most people think about conflict in Newtonian and Freudian terms. Newtonian science explained things by breaking them down into discreet parts, independent of the whole, while Freudian thinking introduced the idea of personality. In today's world, people tend to explain conflict in terms of "personality clashes," and to address persistent conflict by moving people (or swapping out the parts). If you have ever concluded that "the problem" was someone's personality, you were thinking in Freudian and Newtonian terms. These two perspectives fit together nicely, and are widely accepted, which seems to add to their validity. But while both paradigms have merit, they also have serious limitations. They are nonsystemic and prone to victim thinking. The forest is missed for the trees, and criticism of individuals becomes a tunnel vision, with consequences for organizations, families, and the people within them.

In contrast, a systemic thinker seeks to understand how their own behavior is influencing others, and vice versa. Rather than focusing on the other as separate and essentially unchangeable, one focuses on the relationship between "the parts," looks for patterns, and looks for ways to influence the system by changing their own behavior. This is an essential task of self-development and of leadership.

At first glance, it's easy to assume that systems thinking discounts individual accountability. Au contraire! A system is made up of individuals, and therefore change begins with you. Leadership, whether in a family or an organization, requires courage, beginning with the courage to hold yourself and others accountable. Systems thinking clarifies individual responsibility, but shifts away from blaming based on personality.

The damage done by triangulation provides a practical reason to think systemically. Triangulation unchecked is a blame-based pattern that pollutes every corner of a system.

We form a "triangle" with our attention whenever we focus together on anything other than our relationship with the person (or persons) we're with. We focus on topics and things that we share a common interest in, such as sports, or we focus on a work topic (the equipment, the plan, etc.). Whether we like or dislike the object of focus, it can be a bonding experience as well as a practical necessity to focus on things together.

So how is that a problem? Nothing is more stable than a triangle, and the pattern of blame and avoidance can be as strong as cement. Triangulation is the root of the classic "us and them" culture, with groups bonding together in opposition to "them" (mother-in-law and daughter versus husband, the kids and dad versus mom, management versus labor, maintenance versus production, etc.). Blame and defensiveness are fueled in a pattern of triangulation. The pattern becomes an excuse and a crutch, and relationships suffer.

As Friedman puts it, "the basic law of emotional triangles is that when any two parts of a system become uncomfortable with one another, they will 'triangle in' or focus upon a third person, or issue, as a way of stabilizing their own relationship with one another." When people bond by complaining about others, they distance themselves further from the other. As they focus their blame on "them," their ability to see their own part in the dance erodes.

These are difficult patterns to break, because people have a strong urge to identify with someone or something (a group, a team, a religion, a nation, etc.). In other words, triangulation is the core reason why it's so hard to break down silos in organizations and coalitions in families.

To address triangulation, the old paradigm of personality clashes is inadequate. The problem isn't that everyone has a "defensive personality," although when you deal with the individuals, it may seem that way. The problem is systemic: triangulation invites blame, defensiveness, and turf wars.

A groundbreaking study by family systems therapist Salvador Minuchin illustrates the way that triangulation operates as a system. Asthma attacks in children were traced to moments of conflict between the child's parents. When they shifted their focus to the child's attack, the parent's conflict ebbed, thus subtly reinforcing the role of the illness in the family system. The child, of course, was not thinking consciously, "Mom and Dad are fighting. I think I'll have an asthma attack to break it up." And Mom and Dad were not thinking, "Quick, let's reward the child's asthma attack by bonding together." They were each responding unintentionally to emotional cues.

Minuchin addressed the triangulation, and decreased the attacks, by helping the parents work out their issues with each other.

This does not mean that all asthma is rooted in triangulation. But it is a striking example of a system's emotional influence on behavior. In Minuchin's study, as the parents learned to deal with each other more productively, the asthma attacks decreased. Strange but true.

Coalitions within families and organizations require a similar approach. It is human nature to bond through "us and them" thinking and stay stuck in the pattern. Nothing will change unless someone chooses direct communication.

Think about your own triangular patterns. What individuals or groups do you bond with, in relation (probably in opposition) to another individual or group? What do you gain? What do you lose? For example, what aspect of your relationship to the person or persons you are bonding with do you overlook in the process? Are you able to communicate with or understand the person or group you are bonding against? Do you want to change the pattern in some way? How?

Let's look at triangulation from another angle, an angle that most people can immediately recognize in their own lives. Person A has tension with person B, so person A complains to person C about person B instead of talking to person B directly. People commonly label this as gossip (except when they are the one doing it). The key variable here is that person A is avoiding being direct with person B.

Ironically, person C often believes they are helping by "being a good listener." And in many instances, that is true, especially if they are practicing the behaviors you have been working on, and in a manner that encourages directness, as we shall soon discuss. But person C can also easily be reinforcing the problem by providing enough of a relief valve to person A that they feel less compelled to deal with person B directly. Even worse, they may reinforce person A's beliefs about person B by joining in the gossip, which often includes something like this, "You can't talk to person B. It will only make things worse." Often people and groups don't even know they are being complained about. It is kept a secret from the targeted person or group. Such secrets are poison in a family or an organization.

When are you person A, who do you complain about to whom?

When are you person C, who gossips to you about whom?

When you're person A, breaking up patterns of triangulation is relatively simple. All you have to do is notice that you're doing it (complaining about a person or group to a sympathetic ear), stop yourself, and work on your relationships directly with person B. If you choose to let off steam to a third person (person C), do so without tearing down person B, and with the intent of understanding your own reactions and gathering yourself to talk directly with person B.

When you are person C (person A is gossiping to you about person B), you can avoid reinforcing the triangle and help person A take responsibility for their own relationships by applying the following steps.

Let them vent enough to begin calming down, and actively listen while being mindful not to join in or tear down person B in any way. Paraphrase to make sure you really understand, and to help them clarify their meaning (see Appendix A). Work with them to put feedback into non-inflammatory terms: specifics such as "I think I could be making this decision" rather than judgments such as "You're overcontrolling." Encourage them to explore and own their own part in whatever isn't working between them and person B.

When they are able to be specific and less critical, encourage them to be direct with person B. If you have the authority to expect them to be direct, do so, and then support them in their efforts. If not, encourage directness, and then respect their own decision making in the matter. It is, of course, their risk, although the fears that justify avoidance usually prove to be overblown. Don't let yourself get sucked in over and over again, if person A is unwilling to work directly on their relationship with person B.

One of my best customers (we collaborated for 14 years until his retirement) hired me because of wanting to reduce triangulation. As the managing director of a large manufacturing organization, he was tired of listening to his direct reports complain to him about each other. His prior position had been HR director, a role where it is easy to get sucked into emotional triangles. It was after all his role to listen, wasn't it? He began to see that the listening was perpetual and was actually reinforcing the indirectness. With coaching he began to insist that his direct reports talk to each other, instead of complaining to him about each other. Furthermore, he reinforced their directness by insisting that they report back to him within a short timeframe on the outcome of their conversations. Left to themselves, they may have continued avoiding, while looking elsewhere for a sympathetic ear (a new triangle). He also offered to sit in with them if needed or to provide professional facilitation. He had been overfunctioning in both roles (MD and HR), but he didn't swing to the opposite extreme and underfunction.

As Friedman puts it, "… stress on leaders (parents, healers, mentors, managers) primarily has to do with the extent to which the leader has been caught in a responsible position for the relationship of two others. They could be two persons (members of the family, any two sides to an argument) or any person or system plus a problem or goal. The way out is to make the two persons responsible for their own relationship, or the other person responsible for his or her problem, *while all still remain connected.* It is that last phrase that differentiates detriangling from simply quitting, resigning, or abdicating. Staying in a triangle without getting triangled oneself gives one far more power than never entering the triangle in the first place. Many … leaders never get stressed because they intuitively stay of triangles; but that makes them less effective."

Despite initial resistance, the managing director stayed the course and the pattern soon changed, with the leadership managing their differences directly, effectively (as is generally the case, the fear of the conversations proved worse than the conversations themselves!), and cascading the same behaviors down into the organization. The organization became better aligned, and for this and other reasons went on to ever higher performance as measured by their own metrics.

The bottom line is: encourage directness in yourself and in others. According to Dr. John Wallen, the creator of The Interpersonal Gap model (covered in Chapter 9), most conflicts are misunderstandings, not personality clashes, and are reinforced by triangulation.

You can solve your own problems. Breaking up patterns of triangulation is a great place to start. Deal with people directly, encourage them to deal with you, and encourage others to deal with each other. It won't always go smooth, but it beats avoidance and gossip by miles.

HOMEOSTASIS

Every relationship is a complex system, with its own field. In other words, every relationship—between people, between groups, between layers in the hierarchy—is a reinforcing loop. Each of us is part of the behavior we are experiencing from others: the behavior we like and the behavior we don't like. Each system craves stability, even when it is dysfunctional. This homeostasis is very hard to break. People instinctively resist most change. Our reptilian brain, wired to assure our survival, prefers "the devil we know over the devil we don't know." Any change in the environment, even as small as someone taking the seat you normally occupy in a meeting room, triggers a reactive response. At a deep emotional level, people prefer predictability. Change requires recognizing the dysfunctional patterns in the system (such as triangulation), and then implementing patient and persistent leadership toward more productive behaviors. Lasting change occurs when the new behaviors become the new homeostasis/culture.

SELF-DIFFERENTIATION

Systems thinking brings us back to this core leadership concept. Take clear stands, stay connected. As mentioned, most of us gravitate one way or the other. We may be good at driving toward a task or saying what we think whether or not it upsets people, or we may be good at building relationships but not so good at taking stands that risk relationship. People get pulled to one or the other extreme by systemic pressure. The ability to do both simultaneously while being a calming presence in the face of reactivity is the core systems thinking leadership skill.

IF YOU CHANGE INDIVIDUALS WITHOUT CHANGING THE SYSTEM, YOU'LL STILL HAVE PROBLEMS

If you swap out the parts when there is misalignment, the new parts will simply grind against each other. Yet that is the primary approach most management teams take—swap out the parts or rearrange them (i.e., change the structure ... more on this in Chapter 10). Real change requires working on alignment throughout the system, and helping the people at every level think and act systemically (see Chapter 11 for more on alignment). Real change requires a critical mass managing problems with a new paradigm that the leader must clarify and convey.

Section III

Emotional Intelligence and Behavioral Science

This section covers the skills necessary for leading and connecting, including a framework for continuous learning to change habits, increase emotional intelligence, and bring strong awareness and behavioral skills to your interactions.

7

Unlocking Your Mind, Emotions, and Behavior

Ponder the graphic shown in Figure 7.1:

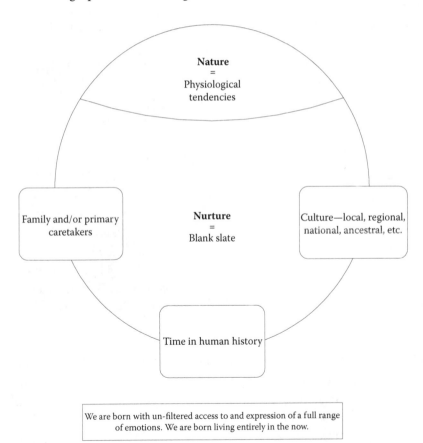

We are born with un-filtered access to and expression of a full range of emotions. We are born living entirely in the now.

FIGURE 7.1
Nature–Nurture. (Drawn by the author.)

You were born, in essence, a blank slate. Yes, there was the influence of "nature"—tendencies handed down by your parents' DNA (the difference between Einstein's brain and my own, for example, the hormonal differences inherent in gender, and so on)—but a growing body of research indicates that "nurture" is by far the greater influence. As Daniel Siegel puts it in *The Developing Mind*, "...all indications point to a primary role of experiential factors..." Our primary caretakers, in the context of their cultural and historical environment, both in terms of shaping our beliefs and at an even more irrational level in terms of how we relate, leave the greatest stamp on who we are.

Consider your beliefs. No one grows up today believing the world is flat, or worshiping Zeus. Attempting to genuinely adopt either of these beliefs would be an exercise in futility. Your current worldview simply won't allow it. Yet if you had been born in a certain place in a certain time, you would have accepted both of those ideas, at least initially, without hesitation.

Like a fish trying to describe water, many of our most fundamental beliefs are invisible to us. As mentioned in the last chapter, two powerful beliefs, reflected and reinforced in the theories of Freud and Newton, hold sway in our current culture. When people have problems at home or at work, they knee-jerk their focus onto parts (Newton) and personalities (Freud). Breaking things down into parts, while a useful exercise for human understanding, ultimately limits that understanding. Physicists have come to understand this, respecting the practicality of Newton's laws, while moving beyond them in understanding the systemic nature of physical phenomenon. As soon as you focus on the particle, you lose sight of the wave. As soon as you focus on the wave, you lose sight of the particle. What you see depends on what you look at. Like the identified patient, the part can only partially be understood without understanding the whole. Non-systemic thinking, when applied to humans, has the same limitations.

Shedding the dominant paradigm and gaining a clear-eyed understanding of yourself and human systems is vital to leading. First, however, let us set the examination of cultural and historical beliefs aside, and look instead at the social process that characterizes each person's initial development as a human being.

Our behavioral and emotional habits emerge primarily through nurture, and are so locked into place by the time we are old enough to notice them, that they seem to be "just the way we are." Some day in the future

I wager that the primacy of nurture will be taken for granted. Today, however, one is likely to encounter an emotional debate if they claim nurture has more impact on our development than nature. This is understandable, given that the last period in which nurture was given primacy resulted in much blame, especially of mothers, even for conditions such as schizophrenia. Especially in the field of mental illness, the popular notion has swung toward biology and chemistry as the root cause. But even clearly physiological conditions are triggered by (or not triggered due to) the emotional and physical environment one is in. And the capacity to cope, or not cope, is rooted in our early precognitive relationships (infants and caretakers).

This need not result in laying blame or in protecting from blame by denying the obvious. There are early patterns that heavily influence each of us, which are well worth understanding, as they are the key to our further development.

Human beings, like the vast majority of mammals, are social animals. As Lewis, Amini, and Lannon demonstrate in their groundbreaking work, *A General Theory of Love*, we need relatively calm and stable attachments to our initial caregivers in order to develop into emotionally stable adults. Indeed, without attachments, infants simply wither and die, even if all their other needs are met. As we shall see, the limbic (or mammalian) portion of our brain literally needs attachment and interaction in order to survive and thrive.

The ability to manage attachments, the first learning process in life (before we have any ability to think), is at the core of emotional health and intelligence. Can you connect without being too needy, or losing your sense of self? Can you maintain distance without being either too anxious or too distant? These dances of togetherness and separateness, noted long ago by family systems guru Murray Bowen, are at the core of social success and strife, both at home and at work.

It is the dance of togetherness and separateness that is at the core of our initial social development. The latest developments in neuroscience substantiate this, documenting the mammalian need for social interaction in order for human beings to survive and thrive during the earliest stages of life. The Holy Roman Emperor Frederick II's ill-fated research in the thirteenth century into what language babies would speak if they were never exposed to the spoken word (he forbade any verbal interaction with the infants in his study) and Rene Spitz's research in the 1940s on infant care wards (the infants were given everything but human interaction) yielded the same results: the isolation of infants leads to death, even if all other conditions (food, water, and shelter) are met.

Similar research with primates substantiates the same conclusions. Without care from a mother, the infant primate declines into despair, viciousness, self-mutilation, and death. Our brains literally get organized through our interactions and cannot develop in a vacuum.

There are four basic patterns to the organization of social relationships that emerge and are passed on generation to generation. These patterns were identified years ago by a renegade psychiatrist named John Bowlby, but only recently backed up by physical science. These are discussed next.

SECURE ATTACHMENT (HIGH TRUST OF SELF, HIGH TRUST OF OTHERS)

This is the result of "ideal" parenting. Before I go on, let me acknowledge that the idea that there is such a thing as an "ideal" approach to parenting may be hard to swallow. I can't help but judge my own parents and my own experience of being a parent (I have two adult sons) when I study this subject. Besides my own emotional subjectivity, cultural influences cloud the topic. But the body of knowledge emerging makes it more and more possible to step back and take a more objective look at the dance of human attachment that begins with birth and plays itself out through life. Again, drawing on Siegel's *The Developing Mind*, one study concerns the adult attachment interviews that are occurring worldwide and have been conducted long enough that infants in the original research have now become parents. They are consistently passing on the attachment behaviors they have developed in relationship to their own parents. Not only are these behavioral patterns proving consistent and reliable, but the theory that humans tend to repeat relationship patterns is also being proven. This reinforces what was already believed in the applied behavioral sciences: objective awareness of one's patterns is essential to further development.

Fortunately, you need not make up your mind about nature versus nurture to benefit from understanding the behavioral patterns identified by attachment theory. Regardless of how we got them, behavioral patterns apply to us all. Let us return to the pattern known as secure attachment. In this model, the infant is allowed enough freedom to explore and develop, while secure in a consistently available parent–infant relationship. They receive comfort when distressed, but are not stifled by an overly anxious adult. Secure attachment results in respect for self and respect for the other. A secure attachment adult is relatively calm when others are intense, has faith in the ability to work things out, and tunes into self and into others with equal ease and skill. In the language of Virginia Satir, they are able to be *congruent*, that is, they are able to convey what is within them when they want to, and able to accurately understand others. These individuals trust themselves (can work independently), trust others (can delegate), and can also work interdependently with ease. They likely have a balanced focus on self and other, and strong capacity for empathy. They are calm when faced with conflict and relationship tensions.

This is a strong relationship orientation from which to lead. Famous leaders through history have had a strong streak of this behavioral set. As we have seen in Chapter 4, apparently divergent leaders such as General George Patton and Mahatma Gandhi share the traits of secure attachment, even though their means to achieving their ends (violence versus nonviolence) sharply contrast. Both were leaders who set clear direction and yet were able to genuinely identify with and connect with their followers without giving in to their followers' fears. Such respect for self, coupled with respect for others, is a solid foundation for leading human systems. As my father likes to point out, Jesus didn't just say "love thy neighbor." He said, "Love thy neighbor as you love yourself." You have to be able to do both.

Does this make a secure attachment leader some sort of flawless human being? Of course not. We all have our foibles and blind spots, some of which emerge from the very traits that make us strong. For example, the secure attachment behavioral pattern could result at times in too much trust in the self and/or the other. Such an individual may not seek or provide expertise and oversight when it is needed, and their trust may occasionally be taken advantage of. The scenarios each of us face are too ambiguous and ever changing for there to be a foolproof way to be. Nonetheless, a tendency of high respect for self and others is the most likely behavioral pattern to create the calm emotional field conducive to high performance. As such, it is a behavioral tendency that is well worth pursuing for both individual and organizational development.

Before describing the remaining attachment strategies, it's worth noting that you may recognize more than one and possibly all four traits in yourself. I certainly do, even though testing (via an instrument called the

"EQ Profile," which is further described in Chapter 8) and my own opinion place me predominately in the secure attachment category. My parents were both quite stable and loving, and the historical period in which I was raised was relatively stable (no wars or natural disasters struck our homes directly, for example), yet no family system is that simple. I have two older siblings, and two younger ones, and with my mom and dad's conflict avoidance during their early parenting years, coupled with dad's frequent absence (for work travel), I was certainly not living in some controlled bubble of parental responsiveness. In other words, it doesn't take dramatic parental dysfunction for an infant to get less than ideal parenting. If you're a parent, then you know that from your own experience. What's important is to recognize the relationship patterns we adapted so we can understand how they impact our current relationships and so that we can intentionally continue our development.

AVOIDANT ATTACHMENT (HIGH TRUST OF SELF, LOW TRUST OF OTHERS)

Avoidant attachment stems from too much independence as an infant. For whatever reason (and there could be millions: another sibling being born nine months later, for example), you had to fend for yourself at times when you would have preferred being comforted and cared for. This is often the fate of firstborns, who tend to become highly self-reliant, both emotionally (by being distant) and in terms of taking charge/responsibility. Adults with this behavioral pattern would likely be highly competitive, and tend toward a win–lose approach to conflict, worrying about themselves and not worrying much about others. Furthermore, it seems likely that avoidant attachment adults would attract anxious attachment adults (see the next category). Likely they will be a very capable person who is only marginally aware of their impact on others, and unlikely to express their emotions and seek soothing, since they didn't get soothed consistently as a child. At work they would be highly responsible and self-motivated performers, but will likely struggle with the requirement of connection if they are in a supervisory position or have interdependent work relationships.

We all project in various ways, to borrow a term from psychology. In other words, whatever our behavioral tendencies, we will rationalize them (they will make sense to us—everyone can explain/defend their own behavior) and we will tend to judge others by our own way of being and thinking. Projection goes further than this and is well worth understanding. For instance, if I'm feeling angry and don't realize it, I may think that you are feeling angry. People tend to focus on others, and blame others for whatever they are projecting. It's easier and more ego gratifying (in a shallow sense) than focusing on oneself. Another common form of projection is for one person to assume that a whole group has the same thoughts and feelings they do, without bothering to find out from the group. This one person can often hijack an entire organization's beliefs about a meeting or a project because they may be the only "feedback," and they may begin to influence others who were not clear about their own stand. That creates another stray cow scenario, and is the reason it is vital to get feedback from the majority present if you want an accurate assessment (this can be done anonymously in five minutes at the end of any important gathering).

But I digress. A challenge at work for a person with avoidant attachment tendencies is that they will expect/project that others will simply function in their own highly independent manner. They will resent needing to provide any more supervision than they would want to receive, and may judge others as flawed if they do not respond to the same minimalist approach. They will likely be better at taking a stand than staying connected, going back to Friedman's model, although they may not see why they should have to communicate where they stand. In other words, their quantity of communication may be considerably less than what is desired by their subordinates and peers. They will expect to be listened to when they do engage, will likely be impatient with listening, and will tend toward debate (trying to shoot holes in ideas or push their own) rather than encourage dialogue (mutual exploration of ideas). Instead of managing performance through regular ongoing conversations, they will likely only give negative performance feedback to a subordinate once their frustration level has grown to a high level of intensity. By then, it will likely be an unsuccessful outcome for either parties. The odds of a person with avoidant attachment tendencies giving positive reinforcement in a timely or regular manner without conscious effort are nil.

The work ethic of a person with avoidant attachment tendencies, the very thing that helps them rise through a system, is a double-edged sword. They trust their own ability to get things done and have a hard time relying on others. They will tend to overfunction in their system, and since most systems are dysfunctional, they will be rewarded for it. They will tend to do work their subordinates should do, for example. The problem becomes not so much their own performance, but rather the underperformance of the rest of the system, which becomes overdependent on their heroic efforts. While reinforced in their behavior, they are nonetheless likely to resent the underfunctioning of the rest of the system, and not see their own role in creating the imbalance.

This is why it is a vital but poorly understood element of self-awareness, emotional intelligence, and systems thinking *to understand one's behavioral patterns regarding trust.* Avoidant attachment tendencies without self-awareness will almost certainly have the systemic impact of Friedman's five characteristics of chronically anxious systems (see Chapter 4), with the ultimate negative outcome of poor performance. A person with avoidant attachment tendencies will have to work hard, and will almost certainly need help, to make adjustments in their behavior. They will only do so of course if they believe the benefits of the effort will outweigh the consequences of staying the same. Their basic task will be to tune in to others by learning the art of dialogue and active listening (see Appendix A), to delegate effectively (see Chapter 12), to work on the root cause of performance improvement rather than simply fighting fires, to give positive and negative feedback in a timely manner (see Chapter 13), and to offer even more information about where they stand (even though they think they have been perfectly clear, others may need more dialogue to truly understand). Over time, if they stick with these and other connection-related behaviors, they will learn to rely on themselves less and trust others more. They will actually rewire their own brains in this direction. It's the essential process that occurs in therapy, but it can occur through any relationships because it is relationship based. Unlike our earliest relationships, from which our tendencies emerged, as an adult we can think about our beliefs and behaviors, and begin to make adjustments.

ANXIOUS ATTACHMENT (LOW TRUST SELF, HIGH TRUST OF OTHERS)

Anxious adults are essentially the opposite of avoidant attachment adults, tuning in to others to preserve harmony in relationships even if the harmony is at their own expense. The simplistic roots of this behavior lie in too much attention from the caregivers during those first couple of years of life. Again, this could be played out in millions of ways, by loving and well-intentioned parents, and is also influenced by birth order. Middleborns, surrounded by their siblings, and lastborns, looking up to their siblings, are more immersed in relationships than firstborns or onlies, and are consequently more likely to take on anxious attachment traits. Whatever the circumstances (both unique and predictable), the infant did not develop an optimal level of trust in self. Instead, they anxiously tune in to others. They will be good listeners, and this will serve them well in terms of connecting, but they will have a hard time taking a clear stand.

They likely will give in to others during conflict in order to preserve relationships, and since they project their own traits as the most reasonable traits, they will quietly resent others for not doing the same. These adults are likely to have high anxiety (worrying about how people feel, for example) and high shame (anger turned inward, "It's my fault"). They will tend to placate, pretending to be happy even when they aren't, or pretending to agree even when they don't. This will soothe both parties in the short term, but is a long-term prescription for resentment and burnout. Adults with anxious attachment tendencies will tend to say yes even when they really need to say no. They will resent that others aren't tuning in to them the way they tune in to others. They will be excellent listeners, but may get paralyzed if they really need to lead.

Again, anxious attachment tendencies without self-awareness will almost certainly have the systemic impact of Friedman's five characteristics of chronically anxious systems. In this case, the anxious attachment person will easily become anxious when the system becomes anxious. Whereas the avoidant attachment person will become a step-up transformer of anger, the anxious attachment person will step up worry and fear in a system. Their basic task will be to calm themselves when they get anxious, and step up more, taking clear and concise stands. Whereas they may be stellar at giving positive feedback, they must push themselves to give negative feedback in a timely manner. Over time, if they stick with these and other related behaviors, they will learn to trust and stand up for themselves more. They will still be skilled at tuning in, but will give in less often. Any kind of change is a lifetime journey, but I have seen many people with anxious attachment tendencies learn to speak for themselves and confront during the T-group-based experiential learning processes my father, my associates, and I conduct, and then continue the behavior once they get a taste of it. In a sense, besides learning from new behaviors that are being modeled for them, they are able to overcome their shame and give themselves permission to stand up for themselves.

Based on similar experiences, and keeping in mind that each individual is unique, I've come to believe that it's easier for an avoidant attachment person to learn to tune in than for an anxious attachment person to learn to step up. The avoidant attachment person, to some extent, only has to learn techniques such as active listening and then consistently apply them to begin to make a real change. The anxious attachment person must overcome fear to take clear stands. This seems to be the tougher task, especially in the work setting, if in a role where the need to lead is ongoing. Both are possible though, and I have been eyewitness to lasting change in the thousands over the past thirty-plus years.

DISORGANIZED ATTACHMENT (LOW TRUST SELF, LOW TRUST OTHERS)

The disorganized attachment adult faces the biggest challenges. Their early childhood environment was somehow so unpredictable that they didn't develop optimal trust in themselves or in others. Without that trust, it is difficult to form and persevere in relationships. A person with disorganized attachment tendencies will easily be overwhelmed with intense emotion when differences surface. They will tend to fall into avoidance behavior, such as keeping to oneself, keeping one's mouth shut, and/or anxiously changing the subject and steering away from tension whenever possible. They will likely harbor a disproportionate amount of anger/blame toward others coupled with feelings of shame/inadequacy toward themselves. They will likely gravitate toward professions where they might essentially be "left alone." They may be bright and highly skilled in such positions, as impaired EQ has no correlation to impairment of IQ. However, such occupations are rare. For example, seemingly standalone occupations such as engineering or accounting place one right into the thick of industrial relationships in a manufacturing environment. In any organization, everyone must relate cross-functionally and to their boss if they are to be effective. And in most organizations, competent individual contributors are promoted into supervision, where they now have to deal with being an authority figure.

These adults will face a very uphill climb if they want to learn to tune into themselves or into others. They will have a hard time staying in relationships and will avoid conflict like the plague. Conversely, once in a dysfunctional relationship, they may stay come hell or high water, no matter how bad the relationship becomes. They will need supportive coaching coupled with a stable long-term work or personal relationship to rewire their brain (allowing time for trust), but it can be done.

In sum, during the first two years of life, the brain gets wired by the dance of separateness and attachment, and then we repeat the pattern habitually throughout life. We can only mature beyond these early patterns by becoming aware of them and then doing the hard work of changing our habits. Like an athlete changing their motion, such experimentation will feel awkward and unnatural. Personality theory fools us into thinking our habits are "who we are." Our reptilian brain, always on the alert for danger, perceives change, *even change we are attempting*, as a threat, and sends the alarm to the emotional and cognitive centers in the brain. We become anxious. We have doubts. It is tempting to give up and go back to what we are used to. This is the challenge with any behavioral change.

Don't give up. Be as accurate about the four patterns (and any and all of your other beliefs and habits) as possible. Push yourself to make small adjustments and not be a prisoner of your patterns. Again, the four attachment theory patterns are

1. Secure attachment (interdependent): High trust of self and others
2. Avoidant attachment (independent): Overly focused on self—low trust of others
3. Insecure attachment (dependent): Overly focused on others—low trust of self
4. Unstable attachment: Low trust of self and others

However, understanding these four patterns, while potentially useful, is not the main point of this chapter. The real message here is that your "personality" is not fixed. Rather, it is a collection of habitual beliefs and behaviors, which you can alter in significant ways. The more accurate your understanding of your beliefs and behaviors, the more you can be the way you want to be. That is the premise upon my claim that *leadership can be learned*. If habit gets in the way of taking clear stands, you can force yourself to take clear stands anyway, and if you stick with it, you will gradually get better at it until it becomes a new habit. If habit gets in the way of connecting, you can force yourself to connect anyway, and if you stick with it, you will gradually get better at it until it becomes a new habit. Recognizing your current habits is freeing. Thinking of your current habits as "who you are" just gets in the way.

Accurate self-awareness is the starting point. You surely agree that achieving as much accuracy about yourself as possible is far wiser than clinging to an inaccurate self-image. With that (and the equally important quest for self-acceptance) in mind, the following is one of my father's favorite quotes, by Thomas Merton:

> Finally I am coming to the conclusion that my highest ambition is to be what I already am. That I will never fulfill my obligation to surpass myself unless I first accept myself—and, if I accept myself fully in the right way, I will already have surpassed myself. For it is the unaccepted self that stands in my way—and will continue to do so as long as it is not accepted. When it is accepted it is my own stepping stone to what is above me. (Merton, 2004)

Let's approach this from a different angle. Again, the source is my father, Robert P. Crosby (shown in action in Figure 7.2), who has been drawing something like Figure 7.3 (below) on flipcharts for decades.

FIGURE 7.2
Robert P. Crosby.

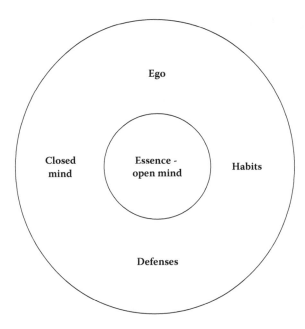

FIGURE 7.3
Ego–Essence. (Drawn by the author.)

Father's graphic only included the words "ego" and "essence." I have added the others. The premise is that our essence is the state we are born in, with a completely open mind and complete congruence between what we feel and what we reveal to others (more on that in the next chapter). With the passage of time, our ego or self-image develops. It is the ego, or self-image, that we are protecting anytime we are defensive or in denial, and anytime we are rigidly attached to our beliefs and opinions. It is not our essence. At our essence remains a completely open mind, the same open mind that learned to walk and talk unhampered by ego (it is ego that worries about how you look when you are trying something new, ego that defends, ego that clings to habits, and ego that closes our mind to new information). An open-minded adult can set aside their ego, reclaim that essence, and unlock their potential.

In the passage from infancy to adulthood, everyone acquires their own unique set of strengths and weaknesses (which are often one's overdone strengths: I'm willing to speak up—I talk too much; I'm thoughtful—I don't speak up enough, etc.). If you trust too much, or if you trust too little, there are consequences. Reclaiming in a conscious manner the open slate you were born with, in terms of objectivity about your beliefs and your patterns of behavior (the aforementioned patterns of trust are just one such example) is vital to both leadership and to your growth potential as a human being. Without an accurate understanding of your habits and a willingness to change, you are unlikely to find the balance of clear stands and staying connected essential to leading.

8

Emotional Intelligence, Crosby Style

Why "Crosby Style?" Because over the course of his career, my father synthesized and applied various theories and sources regarding the role of emotions in interpersonal and organization dynamics, and created a unique approach that I have had the privilege of building on. The word "applied" is important here. Father's "applied behavioral science" method, which I follow, is to test our theories by applying them to ourselves, and through our work with organizations. The model and methods then stay practical because we only keep what survives actual usage.

My father was first exposed to the study of emotion in 1953 when he participated in his first T-group, the group learning process invented by Kurt Lewin. Father's industry adaptation of the T-group has since raised the emotional intelligence of literally thousands of workers (both "white" collar and "blue" collar, often mixed together), and has played an important role in the on-going development of his approach. Along the way, father met John Wallen. Wallen's Interpersonal Gap (covered in Chapter 9) in my opinion is unmatched in terms of teaching skills about emotions and clarifying the process of how we generate emotions within ourselves. Add family systems theory (Bowen and Friedman, in particular) and neuroscience, and father's multi-disciplinary approach evolved into a truly unique framework for emotional intelligence (or "EQ" for short, which means emotional quotient).

In 1995 Daniel Goleman added his voice, popularizing EQ with the publication of his best seller, "Emotional Intelligence." Goleman built on reams of existing research both to provide a model of EQ and to assert that the critical factor in career success is not IQ, but rather EQ.

Building on all of the above, I've come to the following: while high IQ can be a blessing, it can also be a curse if coupled with an inability to connect with others and turn one's ideas into action. For ages, people have unwittingly settled for and even fostered lower EQ by trying to *control* their emotions through denying or ignoring them. Ironically, such an attempt is based on *fear of emotion*, and hence is an emotional/ irrational approach to emotion. Worse, it blinds the individual to important data available from their own "inner guidance system" (more on this later). To the extent one is blind to emotion, one is more likely to act off emotion without understanding the root cause of their actions, such as the patterns of trust we covered in the last chapter. To be rational about one's emotions, one must use their cognitive brain to pay attention to the messages that emotions are providing. Fortunately, science is proving that by working on awareness of emotion in yourself and in others, you don't have to be an Einstein to increase your emotional maturity, which research indicates is a major determinate of success and happiness. As Daniel Goleman pointed out in *Working with Emotional Intelligence*:

- EQ accounted for 67% of the abilities deemed necessary for superior performance.
- EQ mattered *twice* as much as technical expertise or IQ.

Unlike IQ (which is a fixed capacity—we either use it, or we don't, but it can't be increased), whatever your current EQ, with intention and guidance, you can improve. This chapter will clarify the concept of emotional intelligence and provide you with practical and simple tips for self-development.

THREE CORE EQ CAPACITIES

There are three core capacities of emotional intelligence (based on the work of Daniel Goleman):

1. Self-awareness
2. Self-management in emotionally intense moments
3. Empathy (awareness of/connection to others)

CORE CAPACITY #1: SELF-AWARENESS

The first core capacity can be broken down into five subcapacities:

A. Clarity about your own emotions
B. Access to full range of emotions
C. Balance of thoughts, feelings, and wants
D. Ability to separate self from other
E. Ability to separate the past from present

A. CLARITY ABOUT YOUR OWN EMOTIONS

To learn about yourself, it is vital to understand your emotions, and your beliefs about emotions. Most people think that some emotions, such as love, are good, and others, such as defensiveness, are bad. Such beliefs can prevent us from seeing clearly what emotions we and others are experiencing. A more rational perspective is that emotion is not inherently good or bad; emotion is simply a constant part of being human. The question is what we do with emotion. If we are unaware of our emotions, we have less control over their impact on our thoughts and behaviors. When we are aware, regardless of what type of emotion is present, we have more influence over what we think and do.

Especially in emotionally intense moments, it is helpful to be able to name emotions, either in your head or verbally. Brain imaging shows an immediate shift in activity from the limbic (or mammalian) area of the brain to the neocortex (or thinking portion of the brain) when this is done. Again, to be rational, you must pay attention to and be as precise as possible about your own emotions. To strengthen your ability, take the Feeling Description Quiz in Appendix A.

B. ACCESS TO FULL RANGE OF EMOTIONS

You were born with a full range of emotions. Like any infant, you expressed them immediately, without shame. Shame actually played an important role in your development, as you learned what emotional expression was acceptable in your family and culture, and what was not. By adulthood, the socialization process is so set that some of us scarcely realize that we have emotions and the vast majority are blind to one emotion or the other.

All emotions are present for a reason. Shame helps us reduce behaviors that are destressing to others, anger helps us take stands, fear makes us alert, joy gives us vitality. Problems arise not from emotions but from behavior. Problems also arise from "overaccessing" or "underaccessing" specific emotions.

While there are other ways to categorize and name emotionality (such as mad, sad, glad, and afraid), the following graph (Figure 8.1) nicely illustrates the full range of emotions. The graph is from Learning in Action's *EQ Profile*, an assessment tool that dovetails the theoretical approach to EQ presented here. The EQ Profile is unique in that rather than rating oneself by simply answering questions, the respondent rates their immediate emotional reactions to a series of video scenarios. Based on their inputs, a plethora of useful visual and written information is generated (including measurements of trust in self and others, a concept covered in the last chapter). Figure 8.1 shows one person's EQ profile range of emotion result.

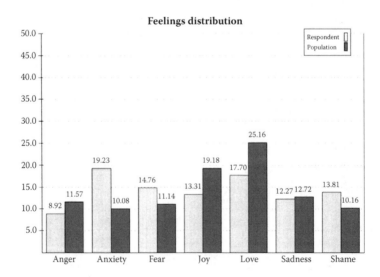

FIGURE 8.1

Feelings distribution. (Used with permission from *Learning in Action Technologies*.)

The distribution divides the range of emotions into portions which together total 100%. The respondent's portions are in light gray; the population that has taken the instrument are the darker bars. This person's distribution reflects relatively high access to anxiety, fear, and shame, coupled with somewhat low access to joy and love. If this is an accurate reflection of their access to emotion (no instrument is 100% accurate, although the EQ Profile does have high validity and reliability), this person may take an overly cautious approach to relationships, both personal and at work. Their low access to anger also correlates to cautiousness or non-assertive tendencies. They may also have low patience with anger in others and tend to ignore their own anger until it takes them by surprise, erupting with high intensity. This, in turn, can become a predictable cycle, with moments of high-intensity anger followed by shame and disruption in relationships, followed again by the habit of "controlling" or ignoring anger while it is small, creating the conditions for the next eruption, and so on.

An opposite profile, if characterized by low anxiety and fear, might lead to being prone to leaping ahead and missing warning signs (i.e., too much trust). Too much access to anger will likely be expressed through blame of others (whereas shame is anger turned against the self) and may very well wear relationships out.

Although some patterns are more common than others, these are just examples of the countless different possible patterns of behavior influenced by EQ. A more balanced access to the full range of emotions can be obtained through conscious effort, and puts you more firmly in the driver's seat regarding emotions in yourself and others.

C. BALANCE OF THOUGHTS, FEELINGS, AND WANTS

Family therapist Murray Bowen, in *Family Evaluation* (with Michael Kerr), describes the highest level of EQ (or, in his words, *differentiation*), as dependent on the degree to which a person is "...able to distinguish between the feeling process and the intellectual process. Associated with the capacity to distinguish between feelings and thoughts is the ability to *choose* between having one's functioning guided by feelings or by thoughts" (Kerr and Bowen, 1988). Without this inner differentiation between feelings and thoughts, one will operate more off emotion, including the emotional cues from one's primary social groups (this includes family, work, and larger entities, such as one's nation). In other words, one will be more prone to "fit in" by only behaving in a manner that is accepted by others, or behave in the opposite extreme—establishing their sense of identity by habitually rebelling. Either states are a form of fusion in family systems theory ... the opposite of differentiation. Even though the fused person will be convinced they are acting independently, they are primarily forming their identity in reaction to others. To be a person who can connect to others, while still respecting their own *inner guidance system* of thoughts, feelings, and wants, it is essential to separate out these three aspects of inner awareness.

To sharpen your own clarity, ask yourself, especially in tense moments:

- What do I want this relationship to be like?
- What outcome do I want from this interaction?
- What am I feeling (mad, sad, glad, afraid, etc.)?
- If my emotional intensity is high, how can I calm myself?
- If my emotional intensity is high, should I postpone this interaction until I am calmer and more able to be the way I want to be?
- If my emotional intensity is high, how much of that has to do with the present, how much my past history with this person, and how much my distant past (my reaction to authority, etc.)?
- How are my feelings effecting my thoughts, and how are my thoughts effecting my feelings?
- Can I see and hear this person as they are now?
- Can I see and hear them as they want to be known?
- What are they thinking, feeling, and wanting?
- What do I really want in this relationship? How do I want to be with them? How do I want them to be with me?
- What am I feeling right now? How is it influencing my thoughts and behavior? What emotion, if any, do I want to convey?
- What do I think about...
  a. This person?
  b. Myself?
  c. What is happening?
- How do I come up with these opinions? What influence is emotion having on my thoughts? What are other possible ways to judge me/them/this situation?

Again, the key here is balance and clarity. If you overrely on wants, you may be impulsive; if you overrely on feelings, you may be irrational; if you overrely on thinking, you may be wrapped up in your own opinions. Here's a more complete version of Bowen's inner guidance system (see figure below).

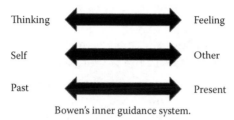

Bowen's inner guidance system.

Differentiation is the ability to sort out and clearly see each of these.

D. ABILITY TO SEPARATE SELF FROM OTHER

Without early attachment, humans, and our closest relatives in the natural world, mammals, wither and die. As the aforementioned tragic early experiences with perfectly sterile infant care wards demonstrated (where most of the infants died), food, water, and shelter are not enough. We are primed for relationships and wired into each other long before we have the capacity to use words. The Newtonian concept that we are essentially separate and distinct entities, applied by Freud and others to the study of being human, has long been challenged by family systems thinking, and more recently by the latest research on the brain. Emotion ripples through relationships, groups, and nations, and even spreads on a global level. When a person in proximity to you becomes tense, it's hard not to become tense yourself, and vice versa. While most communication moves slow as mud, rumors spread in companies like wildfire, riding on a wave of fear. Likewise, when a meeting suddenly lightens up, everyone is likely to feel light. We are more wired together than we have led ourselves to believe.

As mentioned, family systems therapists refer to this as the emotional field. Individuals with high EQ recognize their role in cocreating the field and their vulnerability to it. That person who drives you crazy is partially the way they are with you because you are probably tense if you even *anticipate* running in to them, let alone are actually in their presence. In other words, your own tension fuels their reaction (tension, fear, etc.). Calming yourself by recognizing your own tension while taking slow, deep breaths is one of the surest pathways to creating calmer relationships. This is equally vital when the initial tension is coming from others.

If you can't separate your emotional experience from others, you're like a puppet on a string. They get mad, you get mad. They get anxious, you get anxious. If that is your pattern, break it. Don't indulge in blaming them for "being tense." Be the source of calm for yourself and for others. There are many simple pathways to managing intensity such as deep breathing or thinking of someone important to you who handles difficulties with ease. Take responsibility and calm yourself when the intensity goes up, and you will create better outcomes for everyone involved.

E. ABILITY TO SEPARATE THE PAST FROM PRESENT

The emotional field also involves fusion of the past with the present. Again, neuroscience shows that we are wired for this. The hippocampus, embedded deep in the brain in close proximity to the reptilian brain, begins storing emotional memory before we can even think. Our attachment patterns regarding trust are only one example. We project our emotional experience of our early caretakers onto others, especially important others such as authority figures and spouses, through the rest of our lives. Emotional intensity is a clue that the brain is being reminded of past experiences in the present. These experiences could have been five minutes ago, when you felt offended in a meeting; ten years ago, when you thought a co-worker or boss intentionally humiliated you; or in the first moments of your life. One of the highest EQ skills is to assume that intensity in the present isn't just about the person or persons you are dealing with now, but also what you are carrying from the past. Furthermore, when you are a leader, everyone below you in the hierarchy is wrestling with the same fusion of their past and present when they are dealing with you. As the ancient Mayans used to say, try not to take it personally. Likewise, don't spew your own past intensity on to people in the present. Differentiate between what you are carrying, such as anger at some past authority figure, and what really is about what is happening now. Easier said than done, because we are talking about highly irrational processes here, but a worthy goal nonetheless, with high returns at home and at work.

CORE CAPACITY #2: SELF-MANAGEMENT IN EMOTIONALLY INTENSE MOMENTS

Time to explore the second core capacity, self-management, which is entirely dependent on core capacity #1 (self-awareness). You can't manage what you have no awareness of! Self-management can be broken down further into three subcategories:

A. Recognition of own patterns/habits
B. Capacity to calm/ground self
C. Commitment to continuously increase your range of constructive choices

A. RECOGNITION OF OWN PATTERNS/HABITS

Recognizing patterns is an art that opens many behavioral windows of opportunity. Take a moment and think about the dance that goes on when you interact with others, especially when there's any level of tension. By "dance" I mean predictable patterns. Humans need patterns, and most patterns are fine, or even pleasant (such as responding when someone smiles and says hello); but other patterns cause unnecessary distress.

Any pattern you are in, you helped create and you have the power to alter, but only if you can see the pattern, and your part in it. For instance, in any group you are in, some people are more talkative, some people are less so. The talkative ones often wish the quieter people would talk more, and the quieter people often wish the talkative ones would talk less. But both parties are comfortable with the pattern and like aspects of it (including the predictability—as mentioned, our reptilian brain is focused on survival, so it loves a predictable environment). What they don't like they probably blame on others, thinking occasional thoughts such as "I wish they would speak up for themselves" or "I wish they would let me speak."

Both are trapped in their own victim thoughts, when all either party has to do is recognize their own behavior and how it is fueling the pattern.

Change is unlikely to come in this and other patterns without self-awareness, and then it becomes simple: The talker could stop talking or inquire of the other's thoughts. The quiet person could speak up.

Both acts take courage. Both acts would initially be uncomfortable. Ironically, even if the other person had been wishing things would change, the actual change would put their reptilian brain on alert, and they would likely tense up. Feeling the stress, the person who has chosen to do something different will also go into reptilian brain alert and be tempted to stop and go back to the way things were (a flight reaction). There is a powerful urge to stick with the known and to slip back into the safety of behaviors you have done before.

These are the emotional dynamics underlying "homeostasis." Systems, including systems made up of people, gravitate towards balance. Kurt Lewin called this tendency "equilibrium." We all want a certain amount of the familiar in our lives to keep ourselves from being overloaded. So much so that we are prone to unintentionally undermining the very changes we genuinely want in ourselves and in others. This has been well documented in treating alcoholism. If the alcoholic stops drinking, the family no longer needs to organize their lives around dealing with the alcoholic. The alcoholic's potential health actually stresses the system, as the members are forced to focus their attention elsewhere. The ensuing stress often encourages the alcoholic back to the bottle, despite everyone's genuine wish for change.

Changing, and maintaining, new behavior takes great patience. Even if everyone you know has always wished you were different, they will be stressed if they are forced to relate to you in a new way. You will be tempted to go back to the familiar patterns of the past. You must be patient and endure the initial feelings of awkwardness and uncertainty in yourself and in others if you really want to change.

B. CAPACITY TO CALM/GROUND SELF

As mentioned, the ability to calm down during times of emotional intensity is a tangible and practical EQ skill. Emotional intensity is a physiological state, in which the adrenal gland is pumping stress hormones into the body so as to fully activate the system.

It takes time to deactivate this process. The sooner you notice intensity building, the sooner you begin to intervene, and the easier it is to return to a calmer state. The advantage of catching emotion at a lower level of intensity underscores again the importance of self-awareness. It is far more manageable to deal with feelings of anger, fear, anxiety, etc., when emotional intensity is low. It is far more difficult when emotional intensity is high. Once the intensity is high, it is very tempting to act on emotions. It becomes easy to rationalize, or justify to oneself, being irrational. Once the intensity is high, even when you do catch yourself and begin to de-escalate, it takes longer to clear the hormones from your system, and you remain prone to new escalations of intensity.

Noticing and naming emotions in your head and possibly out loud to others when they are at a low level of intensity is a habit well worth developing. Here again, brain imaging offers good news: your capacity to notice the full range of emotions may have eroded, but you still have the potential. The emotions are still there; it's the neural pathways that have eroded. By focusing your attention on naming the physiological states we call emotions, you can reestablish those pathways, even if you are 110 years old. We can't create new brain cells, but we can activate the ones we've got for the rest of our lives.

Paying attention to emotions when they are small gives you more capacity to choose your behavior. You may choose to let someone know you are serious about something. You may choose to let them know you are happy with something they have done (study after study indicates that people don't hear that enough, either at home or at work). You may choose to do your best to hide what you are feeling. You only have these choices if you are aware of your emotional state.

Paying attention to emotions when they are small has an additional payoff. As mentioned, the very act of describing your emotions, either silently or aloud, shifts the locus of brain activity from the limbic system (or emotional center) to the neocortex. It is an immediate calming technique or, to borrow a term used in the treatment of panic attacks and anxiety disorders, a way to begin "grounding" oneself.

Once you recognize the need, you can further ground yourself with deep breathing, by focusing on tensing and releasing muscles, by firmly planting your feet on the floor, by conjuring the memory of someone you admire, and so on. Google the word "grounding" and you will see that there are endless possibilities. The important thing is to find a method that works for you, and apply it in emotionally intense situations.

C. COMMITMENT TO CONTINUOUSLY INCREASE YOUR RANGE OF CONSTRUCTIVE CHOICES

The final capacity of self-management is simple: Commit to seeking constructive outcomes. Look for ways that support the self-esteem of everyone involved. Look for outcomes that satisfy all parties. Even when a win–lose option seems to be the right path, find ways to support the people who "lose."

Family therapist Virginia Satir constructed a simple model for understanding conflict situations. There is you, there is the other (or others), and there is the topic. An imbalanced focus on any of the three variables decreases the likelihood of a constructive outcome. If I only focus on you, I am likely not being true to myself. If I only focus on me, I am discounting you. And if we only focus on the topic, we are in trouble if what is going on between us is impacting our exchange about the topic. As Friedman, puts it, "people can only hear you when they are moving toward you, and they are not likely to when your words are pursuing them." In other words, if we have put each other off, we aren't likely to be listening, no matter how elegant and/or logical the words. Look for outcomes that respect all three elements, that are mutually satisfactory, and that help set an emotional tone of trust during future moments of conflict.

CORE CAPACITY #3: EMPATHY (AWARENESS OF/CONNECTION TO OTHERS)

Empathy, like self-management, is also dependent on self-awareness. If you aren't able to accurately tune in to your own emotions, you are unlikely to be able to understand and empathize with the emotions of others. Empathy can be broken down further into four subcapacities:

A. Accuracy—Understanding their experience
B. Compassion—Caring about their experience
C. Openness—Respecting/surfacing differences
D. Interaction—Actively demonstrating accuracy, compassion, and an open mind

A. ACCURACY—UNDERSTANDING THEIR EXPERIENCE

This capacity is just what it sounds like. When you attempt to understand what others want, think, and feel, how accurate is your understanding? One reliable way to increase your accuracy is through an active listening skill called paraphrasing. This is not parroting back someone's words, but rather letting them know what you think they mean. For a more detailed description of paraphrasing, read Appendix A.

Perception check, telling a person your hunch about how they are feeling emotionally (also explored in Appendix A), is another means for checking the accuracy of your understanding, with the added benefit of communicating to the other that you are paying attention.

More important than any technique, however, is your intent. Do you want to understand others? Do you see value in it? If so, then practice mindfulness. Clear your mind and give them your full attention. In the words of Pythagoras (580 BC–500 BC), "Learn to be silent. Let your quiet mind listen and absorb" (Dyer, 1998).

Paradoxically, to really listen, you have to be active. Actively listen by paraphrasing and asking questions to make sure you truly understand. If your habit is to focus more on being heard, rather than on listening, control your habit. As Covey (1989) put it, "seek first to understand..." For more on tuning in, read EQ subcategory C. Openness—Respecting/ Surfacing Differences.

B. COMPASSION—CARING ABOUT THEIR EXPERIENCE

In this sense, compassion is literally your ability to put yourself in another's shoes. Not just to understand accurately, but to be able to feel for what they are going through, and convey that you care. The same behaviors that increase empathy accuracy will also help you convey compassion.

As the renowned therapist Carl Rogers put it, if you want to connect you need to be able to convey "genuine positive regard" through your words, facial expression, body language, and tone of voice (Rogers, 1961). If any of these elements send a different message, people will tune into it, especially during times of tension. Even when you do genuinely view them with positive regard and give a consistent message, some may misunderstand. But you can increase the frequency of conveying compassion if you work on it. A great way to learn if you are succeeding is to get feedback at home, at work, and from professionals.

Without consistently conveying compassion, you are unlikely to earn the respect necessary to influence others or to lead.

―――――――――

C. OPENNESS—RESPECTING/SURFACING DIFFERENCES

Many people are so uncomfortable with differences that they either quickly change the subject in order to maintain "peace," or they lock into debate mode in order to protect their own egos. Both habits potentially damage relationships and limit the quality of communication.

If your habit is to avoid, the path forward is to be aware during moments of intensity, ground yourself, and engage both through active listening and by conveying what you want, think, and feel.

If your habit is to slip into discussion/debate, the path to more constructive behavior again starts with awareness. According to systems thinker Peter Senge, in his *The Fifth Discipline*, "discussion... has its roots with 'percussion' and 'concussion,' literally a heaving of ideas back and forth in a winner-takes-all competition."

Both parties are working hard, perhaps without even realizing it, to ensure that their way of thinking is the right way of thinking, or the right way to proceed. In a discussion, people tend to listen only enough to gain ammunition from what the other is saying. They aren't listening to understand. Their ego is attached to whatever they are trying to get across, and if the other party doesn't accept it, it will be a blow. Both may feel injured by, and indignant about, the other's behavior. Instead of listening, both are spending most of their time formulating their next statements while the other is speaking, and may have worked on their opening statements for hours or days prior to the interaction. It's almost like there are two monologues going on simultaneously, with each party only pausing while the other speaks, and doing their best to look attentive while they occupy themselves with what to say next.

Ironically, both care so much about being heard that the odds of either getting their message across are low, since neither are focused on really listening. At the end of a discussion, the participants often "agree to disagree," since they realize that they are getting nowhere. They are likely to part ways frustrated, both believing (and probably being correct) that the other didn't get the message, and both blaming the other for being unreasonable.

It is a cocreated waste of time and energy, damaging to any relationship. It is also common practice.

The alternative to discussion is simple. The first step is to notice the pattern. The second step is to choose to be different in the interaction. The key difference, as Covey's full quote puts it, is to "seek first to understand, than to be understood" (Covey, 1989). Don't "seek to understand" as a means to an end (i.e., as a clever way to get them to listen so that you can get back to the agenda of being understood). You'll distract yourself if you aren't genuine in your intent. Do your best to really understand the perspective of the other as an end unto itself. Clear your thoughts and listen. Stop preparing your next statements. Trust that you will know what to say if you need to say something. Paraphrase, paraphrase, paraphrase! What are they really trying to say? Put yourself in their shoes. What's the whole picture of what they're trying to put across, including, perhaps, the difficulties they may be having dealing with you? Set your ego aside! Make sure that you really understand and that they can see it.

You will learn things this way, and they may—and I mean "may," not "will"—also want to understand you in return. But don't get caught up in "needing" that. Seek to understand, and it's likely you'll find the experience of understanding is its own reward.

Senge calls a two-way focus on exploring each other's ideas and perspective "dialogue." In his words, "the word dialogue comes from the Greek dialogos. Dia means through. Logos means the word, or more broadly, the meaning...the original meaning...was...a free flow of meaning between people." This is a rich experience when reciprocated, but you will only have such reciprocal experiences, dancing the dance of dialogue, if you start with yourself and genuinely work to understand the other. In discussion, people are consumed with getting heard. In dialogue, people focus on making sure they understand. This is critical to the leadership art of connecting.

D. INTERACTION—ACTIVELY DEMONSTRATING ACCURACY, COMPASSION, AND AN OPEN MIND

The final subcategory is given life by mixing the behaviors of accuracy, compassion, and openness (as described above).

In short, emotional intelligence is a disciplined awareness of and respect for emotion in self and in others, which in turn allows for more rational management of emotional moments. EQ is, in essence, about relationships. Individuals with low EQ, even if they have high IQ, will almost certainly have trouble at work and in their personal lives due to difficulty relating to others.

CHARACTERISTICS OF WELL-DEVELOPED EMOTIONAL INTELLIGENCE VS. UNDERDEVELOPED EMOTIONAL INTELLIGENCE

Above all else, the fundamental challenge is to know oneself and to work to overcome one's blind spots and habitual patterns of behavior. In an ideal sense, a person with high EQ has consistent awareness of even low intensity emotion, combined with a balanced experience of the full range of emotions. A healthy balance includes a high proportion of emotions that increase energy such as joy and love, but also appropriate doses of anger, fear, sadness, shame, and anxiety.

If the idea that those last five emotions are part of the ideal surprises you, consider this: judging some emotions as "good" and others as "bad" is irrational. Humans are wired with all emotions for a reason. If you have no shame, you'd be shameless; if you have no fear, you'd be reckless. Trouble doesn't come from having emotions such as anger, but from acting on them without realizing it. Trouble also comes from *imbalance*, where a person is operating off of a limited range of emotions. They will be driven by emotion in ways they are unaware of, and reactive to emotion in others. They may fool themselves by not appearing "emotional," but the need for such a facade is in itself an emotional and limiting reaction.

A person with high EQ also has a strong dose of optimism tempered with some healthy pessimism. They have a balanced ability to focus on self and on others, especially during tension, with clarity about what each wants, thinks, and feels. That, of course, requires the capacity to empathize accurately and with compassion. Imbalance, deficiencies, and blind spots in any of these areas decrease one's self-knowledge and one's capacity to know and understand others.

At work, a person with high EQ will take responsibility for their own well-being, clearly conveying what they want, think, and feel when they so choose, while tuning in and helping others to clarify the same. They will be able to have rational conversations about anything.

A wise leader will invest in their own EQ and the EQ of their organization to decrease drama, and increase satisfaction and productivity. This is especially important between supervisors and their subordinates. Research shows time and again that the reporting relationship is the most important in the workplace, and the one that needs to be developed to assure performance. Bosses and subordinates with low EQ are more likely to act on emotion without realizing it, blame others for their emotional states, repeat self-defeating patterns of interaction, and create needless havoc in organizations. The negative effect becomes amplified the higher the person rises.

> The positive intent of authority is to get things done. The negative intent and frequent consequence is to run roughshod over people. The positive intent of consensus is to significantly involve people in decision-making. The negative intent and frequent consequence is to stifle action and give power to the most stubborn. The intertwining of the positives is what (Emotionally Intelligent Leadership) is about.
>
> **Robert P. Crosby**

9

Behavioral Science—
The Interpersonal Gap

Applied behavioral scientist Kurt Lewin, the founder of my profession (organization development), once said "There's nothing so practical as a good theory" (Lewin, 1951). *The Interpersonal Gap* (by John Wallen, 1964) is one of the most practical theories of behavioral science, offering a transformational mix of awareness and behavioral skills. Self-awareness and the ability to tune in to others is a foundation of personal effectiveness, but awareness without skills is like a puzzle with half the pieces missing. By logically packaging awareness and skills in a practical manner, Wallen's theory perfectly supports both EQ and Friedman's leadership model.

According to Wallen, "The most basic and recurring problems in social life stem from what you intend and the actual effect of your actions on others" (Wallen, *The Interpersonal Gap*). I would add (and I'm confident Wallen would agree) that "basic and recurring problems" stem equally from the reverse: your own interpretations, sometimes accurate, sometimes not, of the intentions of others. While both their interpretation of you and your interpretation of them are worth paying attention to, it is the latter source of trouble over which you have the most potential control.

In short, Wallen's theory is that each of us has intentions in every interaction (we intend a certain impact), we translate (or encode) our intentions into words and actions, the people we are interacting with translate (decode) our words and actions, and the decoding determines the initial emotional impact on the receiver, as illustrated in Figure 9.1.

This process occurs constantly, and in a nanosecond. I react to you, and in that moment you are already reacting to my reactions. To further complicate things, our filters are complex and ever changing. Our history together, our separate life experiences, our culture, the nature

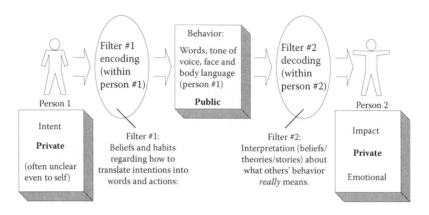

FIGURE 9.1

Interpersonal gap. (Graph drawn by the author using Visio, concept created by Dr. John Wallen, accessed through the public domain.)

of our relationship (i.e., roles such as boss and subordinate, parent and child, salesperson and customer, etc.) all impact our immediate filters about each other. There is ample potential for misunderstanding at any step in the process (beginning with the formidable task of understanding yourself—that is, with having clarity about what impact you really want in any given interaction). Such misunderstandings are what Wallen refers to as a "gap." As he puts it, "Interpersonal gap refers to the degree of congruence between one person's intentions and the effect produced in the other. If the effect is what is intended, the gap has been bridged. If the effect is the opposite of what was intended, the gap has become greater."

Wallen goes on to say, "We see our own actions in the light of our own intentions, but we see the other's actions not in the light of the other person's intentions but in the effect on us." In other words, we usually know what we intended, especially when we believe we've been misunderstood (when we believe others have interpreted our words and actions differently than we intended). It is easy to notice Wallen's gap in those moments. That awareness is the first vital step in potentially clearing up such misunderstandings.

It's more problematic when the shoe is on the other foot: when you interpret another's words and actions in a manner that has an undesired effect on you.

Understanding the power your interpretations have on your own reactions is the starting point for increasing your objectivity and becoming less of a victim to your own interpretations. For example, a person who gives you "close supervision" (an interpretation in itself) may also be decoded/interpreted as (a) "not trusting your work" or (b) "being committed to you," [or (c), or (d), etc.]. A worker who speaks with anger may also be decoded/interpreted either as (a) "a troublemaker" or (b) "passionate about their job." The same behaviors, decoded differently, evoke different reactions (emotions, beliefs, etc.). Simple but hard to remember when the (emotional) heat is on, especially since your circle of associates will likely agree with your negative interpretations, lending what seems like validity to your judgments about the other person or group (thus reinforcing the systems dynamics of herding, triangulation and homeostasis). And the subtle tension fueled by such negative beliefs makes it likely that future interactions will further reinforce the current outcomes.

Does this mean that you should never have negative judgments of others? Absolutely not. Besides the fact that such a suspension of interpretation would be virtually unachievable, it would be undesirable as well. Honest and timely critical feedback is a vital factor in a high-performance workplace (more on this important topic in Chapter 13). What it does mean in a nutshell is that it is wise to avoid using needlessly inflammatory judgments ("You're not a team player"), while it is useful to be as skillful as possible in describing the behavior that led to your interpretations of others (especially if you are an authority figure giving them performance feedback!). Equally important, it is wise to leave ample room for questioning your interpretations.

In other words, don't get so attached to your interpretations that you defend them and close your mind to other possibilities. If you are being objective, you will understand that your initial interpretation of someone's words and actions may be very different than what they meant. Close gaps by being specific about what you think they said or did (keeping in mind that they may not describe their words and deeds the same way), and about the emotional impact your interpretation of their words and actions is having on you. The good news is you have the ability to reconsider your own interpretations, and that is a critical step for breaking any patterns of misunderstanding that are needlessly complicating your relationships at home and at work.

Wallen states: "I know myself by my intentions; I know others by their____."

How would you finish the sentence? Think of your response, and then continue reading.

If you said, "I know others by their actions/behavior," your answer reflects the dominant cultural perspective of our times. In other words, most people would give that answer. It is part of the personality theory culture we spoke about earlier. "I know them by their actions; for things to be different, they have to be different." It follows that your efforts will be on analyzing them and trying to change them (or getting rid of them). And since the people around you are operating in the same cultural mode (answering the question the same way), that seems to validate your perspective. It also means that when there is tension, it is likely they will be analyzing your personality flaws, similar to how you are analyzing them. This cultural paradigm does more damage than good.

Wallen's completion of that sentence, on the other hand, is a radical shift. "I know myself by my intentions. I know others by my interpretations." I know you by the stories I *make up* about what I believe your words and actions *really* mean. This leads to increased responsibility and to an empowering possibility. If I change my stories, I change my reaction. In other words, I create my own reactions. A subtle shift, but radically different than popular belief. "You made me angry!" Nope. "I interpreted your words and actions as an attack, as an attempt to thwart what I want, and my thoughts aroused anger within me." And if one is really objective they might add, "And frankly, there's a good chance I misunderstood what you meant to convey."

"I know you by my interpretations" is both a sobering and calming perspective. Rather than believing, defending, and reacting to your own interpretations, if you maintain awareness of the possibility of misunderstanding (an awareness that will have a grounding effect), you open the door to more rational relationships—you will calm yourself and put your thinking mind in charge.

Let's look at the interpersonal gap from yet another angle. To understand your own reactions and to convey useful feedback to another, it's important to be as clear as you can about what "action" you are interpreting. When you are conversing with someone, what sort of behavior are you taking in?

For our purposes, there are three primary sources of behavioral information: words, body language, and tone of voice. Words are what the person is saying and what you are hearing them say (which may be two different things!). Body language is constant and includes the powerful information conveyed by facial expression. Are they smiling? Frowning? Looking at you? Leaning toward you? Leaning back? Tensing their muscles? Slumped in their posture? Folding their arms? All body language provides information about the sender of the message, and is open to interpretation by the receiver. Last, but not necessarily least, does the tone of voice match the words being conveyed? Think of the various tones that could be used with the words "Thanks a lot." As you can probably surmise, very different messages can be conveyed, depending on the tone.

A famous study by Dr. Albert Mehrabian assessed where the receiver tuned in for understanding, when the messages from these three aspects of behavior (body, tone, and words) were inconsistent. Mehrabian's research breaks them down into percentages. What percentage do you think you get the message from when there are mixed messages from the sender? Take your best guess, and then see below:

Body language:_____%
Words:_____%
Tone:_____%

In Dr. Mehrabian's research, these were the percentages (Mehrabian, accessed through the public domain):

Body language: 55%
Tone: 38%
Words: 7%

If you answered differently, that doesn't invalidate your answer. You may be getting more of your information from one or two of these sources than did the people in the study, or you may be closer to the study's numbers than you realize. Either way, your ability to be specific about what you are reacting to will increase your own clarity about your reactions and improve the clarity of the feedback you give to others. For example, when you believe you are receiving a mixed message, you could think or say something like this: "When you said you were happy, you were frowning, so I didn't believe it." Compare that to somebody being effected by the same behavior, and thinking or saying, "liar." Feedback that primarily conveys specific behavior is generally less inflammatory than feedback that primarily or solely conveys judgments (interpretations). It's also more likely that the receiver and the sender can learn from and act on behaviorally specific feedback. The ability to give behaviorally specific feedback, free of interpretations, is essential if you are in a position of supervision, and important at home if you want less fighting and more understanding. Frankly, if you can't be behaviorally specific, you are better off not saying anything at all. How you put things and what you focus on does matter. Again, we'll explore the topic of giving and receiving feedback in more depth in Chapter 13.

You can also pay attention to the alignment of these three variables in your own communication. How aware are you of your own facial expressions? Do you smile when you are anxious or delivering a serious message? Many people smile because they are afraid of how the message will be received. Others cover their inner state by never varying their expression. Unfortunately, either behavior is likely to be confusing to the person on the receiving end. And neither behavior protects you from conveying *something*, sometimes conveying messages very different than what you intended. Ironically, people who have a more or less consistently blank facial expression, especially if they are in positions of authority, are often misinterpreted more, because people have less to go on and are filling in the blanks with their own imaginations (and with authority figures, they often imagine the worst).

If you want people to get a clear message, try smiling when you like what's happening, and looking serious when you feel serious. Family therapist Virginia Satir calls this match between your inner experience and your outer expression "congruency." As mentioned earlier, we all started life that way. When you were happy you looked happy, when you were sad you looked sad, and so on. If you have ever been around an infant, you know this to be true. From that point on, we all learned habits of what to show and what not to show. Through persistent intentional effort, you can unlearn those habits that are no longer serving you well, and relearn how to be congruent when you want to be.

The same is true of tone, and of words. As the Toltec Mayans have known for thousands of years, your words are powerful. Endeavor to say what you mean, and mean what you say. Be kind with your words, to yourself (in your head), and to others. Keep your word.

Wallen identified four ways to close interpersonal gaps. Read Appendix A and experiment with them. Remember, not every experiment will go the way you want it to. Learning new behaviors can be awkward, and the people you are with may not know what to make of your efforts. But just because you fall down doesn't mean learning to walk is a mistake. If the voice in your head starts being negative the first time you try new behavior and the interaction doesn't go the way you want, challenge that filter!

It might be with you the rest of your life, but you don't have to listen to it! Thank goodness that filter is a learned habit and wasn't in place when you were learning to walk and talk! You can stumble and still move forward. It doesn't mean that you, or the method, is a failure. Be clear about what you want, and go after it. The more you try on the behaviors in this book, the more you'll forge your own path, your own style, and create more of what you want at home and at work.

Section IV

Leading and Managing

Despite much hype to the contrary, my experience makes it clear that leaders must lead *and* manage. Yes, one can overmanage (or micromanage), and that's to be avoided, but leaders who think they can set a direction and then let go are even less likely than micromanagers to get the results they are looking for. This section explores how to lead *and* manage.

10

Stability Is Good

Along with the hype that leading and managing are two completely separate roles (instead of complementary functions of the same role, as I am advocating), another fad hyped since the 1980s has been that "change is good." Leaders and employees alike have been admonished to "embrace change." As fads go, this one has been enduring, partially because change is *indeed* constant, and partially because the need to manage change has been highlighted by the challenges of IT implementations, where costly and disappointing outcomes are more likely than not. Among the latest in a long string of research documenting such disappointing outcomes is the July 2008 study by the US Government Accounting Office (GAO) that found that of 840 federally funded projects, 49% were poorly planned, poorly performing, or both. In case you are tempted to conclude that the situation is better in private organizations, a 2008 study by the Information Systems Audit and Control Association found that 43% of 400 respondents admitted that their organization had had a recent project failure.

My own track record, based on the leadership and change models taught here, is much more successful. My father, my colleagues, and I have a consistent history of successful change management, including helping decrease the length of nuclear refueling outages at PECO Nuclear, helping a software organization release their next upgrade on time and on budget (after their prior release had been disastrously late), facilitating a multinational Oracle implementation, as well as many other IT and non-IT examples. The same principles of high-performance leadership apply to managing change, especially goal clarity (next chapter), single point accountability for all tasks and decisions (much more on this in Chapter 12), role clarity, the need for both clear stands and for well-organized engagement of the people who will be effected by the change (plant managers, end users, etc.), visibility of roles, tasks, and deadlines, and careful monitoring and support. In other words, *lead the change, manage the process.*

The same holds true for daily operations. Leaders must lead (take clear stands and connect), and they must manage. As President Reagan put it, they must "trust but verify." Of course, if there are layers and cross-functional silos, they are going to delegate much of the task of monitoring, but they must monitor the monitoring. To simply say "here's where we are going" and then to detach completely from what happens next is only going to work by luck and on rare occasions. Don't be like Napoleon at Waterloo. Leaders must manage, and every manager must lead to be effective.

There is no cookie cutter here. You have to figure out how much freedom to allow and how much oversight to provide, and you have to work through the wants and reactions of your subordinates regarding how much "managing" is too little or too much from their perspective. You must listen to your own inner voice and to the voices of your people, and then decide. As time passes, you must adjust and renew the way you manage based on whether you are getting the desired results. And since you want results (surely), the management of daily tasks is also the management of change. You may have output goals (such as keeping troubled youth in school, or producing a product at or below a certain cost) that remain the same over time, but you will always have process and other types of performance improvement opportunities in any type of daily operation. Managing *is* managing change.

Hence the title of this chapter. To get high performance and continuous improvement, *embracing and creating stability is at least as important as embracing change.* Quality and Lean (which both have roots in Lewin's action research) methods require process stability in order to assure orderly and reliable continuous improvement. Ambiguity is inevitable in life and work, but the more clarity that can be provided about tasks, decisions, roles, etc., the easier it is to execute at a high level of performance. Both neurological and organizational research supports this. It has been said that it takes groups approximately two years to get to a high level of performance following every leadership change. The US Navy's research indicates a significant performance dip for up to six months every time a leader changes (Figure 10.1).

Neuroscience shows us that our brains are wired to go on alert when there are changes in the environment (again, as small as someone sitting in the chair you normally sit in at a regular meeting). The amount of change in most of the organizations I've been in (and that is quite a few since the beginning of my career back in 1984), some by circumstance (leaders

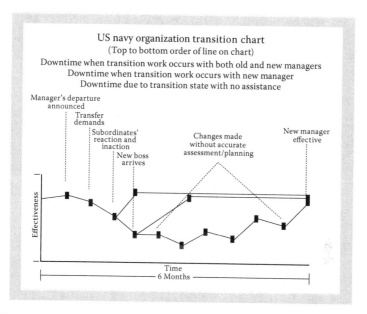

FIGURE 10.1
Transition state.

retire, markets shrink, etc.), much by choice, is overwhelming. No wonder research shows that morale is low in most organizations! People are too stressed, and again turning to research, there is good stress (the sense of responsibility to get the job done and to do it well, the focus of a sports team), but there can clearly be too much stress. The results, as illustrated by Friedman's Five Characteristics (covered in Chapter 4), is predictable: dysfunction increases and performance declines.

Friedman's "quick fix mentality" (again, in Chapter 4) is part of the problem and is a leadership dilemma/responsibility. Implement improvement initiatives absolutely. But for heaven's sake, don't tackle so many improvement initiatives at the same time that you overwhelm your people and screw up not only the initiatives but daily operations as well.

Equally important, don't blame your people for being stressed. Stress is a physiological response (triggered in the primitive brain) to change. People don't need to go to training classes to figure out how to "embrace change." Sending them to such a class, or handing out books on how to handle change, implies that managing change is primarily a matter of attitude. As in all things, how each person manages themselves *is* always part of the picture, but change is primarily a leadership issue in organizations and focusing on it as a personal issue can add insult to injury.

What people really need is calm leaders who will be patient with the initial stress reaction, and who will stay the course (unless presented with compelling and overwhelming evidence that the course is likely to be disastrous, then you would be wise to not pull a Burnside! Change your course!), while allowing as much real influence on how to implement as possible. Create as much clarity as possible about what can be influenced, and what is beyond influence, and then create clear ways to allow your people to influence what they can. The more they are engaged, the less stressful and the higher quality the change will be.

Equally important, be selective about the changes you are choosing. Pick changes that make sense to your people if possible, changes that they have been requesting and/or that are clearly targeted at removing barriers to performance and morale. When you believe you must impose change that will not be popular, don't chastise them. Acknowledge their feelings and work calmly on how to engage them as much as possible. If at all possible, don't overdue the number and frequency of such changes.

One organization I worked for was moving from a culture of almost no changes. People had worked in the same departments, locations, and functions for years, and thought they always would. To say the least, they were heavily siloed. To change the culture and create more cross-functional interaction and perspective, the organization began forcing people to move into different locations and functions (engineers to operations, and so on), and to move laterally and up much more frequently so that groups would have new leaders, and leaders would head new groups. No longer would groups have the same leader for decades, with change only occurring at retirement. It was not going to happen by itself, so forcing such movement made sense.

The organization, however, went overboard in many cases, and created unnecessary chaos during a time of a great many other the changes. One of my functions was to facilitate leadership transition conversations between groups and new leaders. Such conversations can rapidly speed the process of establishing new clarity about roles, expectations, etc., thus moving the team quickly towards a new period of relative stability. In the span of four years I facilitated five such conversations for one young leader, as he was reassigned to five different groups! Capable as he was, there was no way that a leader of any of those groups was able to meet their potential of high performance. It was simply too much change too soon.

Needless change is an epidemic. In 1995, my father wrote an article called, "Organizational Structural Change: A Trap or a Path?" The organization he had worked for in the 1960s had changed its structure three times in eight years. As he put it, "The next time someone suggests a major structural change as a solution, ask yourself, 'Is making and remaking the structure a pattern in this company?' If the answer is 'yes,' look elsewhere for a path." Structural change, like leadership transitions, has consequences (confusion about roles, new silos replacing the old, etc.). Most organizations overuse it to attack cross-functional problems. Engineering is decentralized to get it closer to the internal customers. Engineering is centralized (often in the same organization a relatively short time later) to assure that solutions are the best for the entire system (not too driven by local internal customers) and that knowledge can more easily be shared between the engineers. Centralization also often occurs in hopes of saving money: everyone will use one centralized group, often outsourced, to reduce the costs of having their own resource. You can substitute "engineering" for any other function (IT, HR, maintenance, etc.) and the same dynamics hold true.

The problem is every structural change creates a certain amount of chaos, and many organizations pile on one structural change after another in rapid succession. By the time the workforce gets orientated to the latest change, they are often confronted with another. Change burnout becomes a real issue, on top of the inevitable confusion. And while one problem may get solved, such as reducing IT costs, another emerges, such as the inability to get needed IT service, which has potentially huge hidden costs.

Cost savings aside, the changes are usually attempts to solve cross-functional problems. Yes, moving the engineers out into the other departments will likely result in engineering solutions more tightly attuned to daily operational needs. That is a worthy goal. But that goal and all cross-functional challenges could be addressed in other ways, without changing structure and/or reporting relationships. The organization can make getting engineers into the field a bigger priority, or if the function is already decentralized, the organization can prioritize time for the function (in this case the engineers) to collaborate with their peers and to work on systemic solutions.

Structures will enable some things and inhibit others. Structural change is at times wise, but it is no doubt an overdone solution and thus in many cases, a needless change, working against the stability that is essential to high performance.

Every structure has its downside. A perfectly flat structure will decrease the bureaucracy that comes with layers, but it will increase the complexity of clarifying who decides what. No matter what the structure, there will be silos. Every group has a tendency to herd together, and must work to overcome isolation and the temptation to blame other groups and locations for cross-functional difficulty. A wise leader has every group working on continuous improvement of their role in each cross-functional process through dialogue and metrics to assure they are giving and receiving what they need on time and in a quality manner.

The idea of the cross-functional or matrixed organization as something new is yet another fad. Organizations and project teams have always been cross-functional, unless everyone in them has the same function for crying out loud. Whether a new group (for a project) or an old cross-functional interdependency (maintenance and production), what is needed is as much goal clarity as possible (such as the cross-functional process metrics mentioned above) and as much role clarity as possible. While some of the role clarity needs to be traditional and task based (who is responsible for what), we find a modified version of Daryl Conner's "Sponsor, Agent, Target" roles also quite useful.* However, one must think differently about these "roles" if they are to be applied effectively. These roles are constantly happening, and at any given moment a member of the system may wear multiple hats.

Contrary to popular usage of the term "sponsor," in our model a leader can only sponsor the activity of their direct reports. If you (the agent) are not getting what you need from a person or group that you are dependent on (the target), then work it respectfully at the lowest level. But if the problem persists, then work for alignment with the sponsor of the targets (their immediate supervisor) and so on up the food chain possibly to a single point above you if none of the layers in between can achieve alignment. Underperforming cross-functional processes are another epidemic in organizations, which are often handled clumsily through personnel and structural changes that don't directly address the process issues (and create more of the chaos of change).

---

* Originally modified by my father, and recently elaborated on by my brother, Chris Crosby, in his book *Strategic Organizational Alignment*.

Project teams underperform for the same reason. A project manager is "put in charge" of people that don't actually report to them. If there is no alignment with the people they actually report to, and misalignment in the layers above, then the resources will often be distracted by other priorities and problems will ensue. Executives responsible for "sponsoring" (by which organizations mean "championing") an initiative across the organization face the same dynamics. Despite their official title, in this model they are just agents who would be well advised to work on alignment with their peers and on alignment up the hierarchy to a single point above their peers (whether that is the next layer or higher) prior to implementation. They would also be wise to engage in and monitor the cascading of alignment from their peers down each layer to the lowest targeted point in the hierarchy. They cannot boss these layers. They can only be boss/sponsor to their direct reports. Creating alignment takes time. Pressing forward without alignment wastes even more time and causes needless conflict and underperformance.

Creating relative stability in terms of role clarity, etc., is no easy task! There is, however, no magic alternative. As a leader and a manager, clarity and relative stability must continuously be sought after and established anew. Goal clarity and alignment is an important ingredient in that quest. Read on as my brother and colleague, Chris Crosby, discusses this challenge and opportunity.

11

Goal Alignment

INTRODUCTION

A colleague of mine recently posted an article titled "Continuous Improvement May Lead to Mediocrity." It's a valid point. Continuous improvement methods can inadvertently become just another effort in a firefighting culture if they are not tied to an effective big picture strategy. I fear, however, that his catchy title will be misinterpreted beyond being a wise caution and instead become another management fad such as "focus on your core business" (which led to companies shedding profitable businesses that were "outside of their core") or the aforementioned "embrace change." The latter has become a non-behaviorally specific performance expectation in many companies and has given rise to countless trainings encouraging employees to "get over resistance to change" as if it is simply a personal issue. A more systemic and non-blaming approach would be to effectively engage people in planning and implementing change. Likewise, rather than abandoning continuous improvement altogether, a much better approach is to combine system-wide continuous improvement with visionary goals that are actually meaningful.

Case Study—As mentioned in Chapter 2, in 2002 the managing director of the Jamalco bauxite refinery's vision was to go from the highest cost producer of alumina in the global Alcoa system to tied for the lowest (he was satisfied with tying two much larger Australian refineries that had huge advantages in terms of scale). He described this stretch goal to a cross section of his refinery employees, including 50% hourly, on a simple flip-chart with the believable message that the highest cost producer was a not a good position to be in if the larger corporation decided to cut costs by closing locations. He then effectively engaged them in continuous improvement, targeted at reaching the broader vision. To do this, he started with a highly structured planning session that outlined a series of initiatives that were deemed critical by the employees in order to achieve the vision. The initiatives, such as a reduction in raw materials lost through leaks, were often led by hourly workers and resulted in huge sustainable savings. The refinery achieved their goals within a year. Then, through continuous improvement, they sustained their position in the cost curve, and were the only refinery in Jamaica to stay open at full production throughout the Great Recession.

In sum—don't throw the baby out with the bath water. Find real and meaningful stretch goals and align your system around the improvements that are critical to achieve them.

This chapter gives advice on doing exactly that. It is an excerpt from my colleague and brother Chris' book, *Strategic Organizational Alignment*, and it is a practical application of Friedman's leadership model. To align the organization, you must take clear stands and connect.

GOAL ALIGNMENT

Scenario 1

Plant manager 1: "We are currently losing money in the market. It costs us $1.48 per pound to make aluminum ingots and we sell them for $1.36 per pound. If we do not lower the cost of making ingots, we are in trouble as a business. In nine months, our goal is to reduce the cost of producing a pound of ingots to $1.21."

Scenario 2

Plant manager 2: "We are not doing so well, we have to improve."
Consultant: "What business metrics are you working toward?"
Plant manager 2: "Metrics? Hmm, not really sure."

The fundamental task of business leadership is to align employees in the same direction. Workplace goals represent that direction. Effective goals are clear, simple, numeric, and measurable. The ability to set simple numeric measurements is an important step in organization alignment. By setting these measurements, you give your employees an easier way to see how what they do contributes to the greater good of the organization. This, in turn, helps them to more fully participate in workplace improvements. Without such clarity, they are more likely to be reduced to people doing tasks disconnected from the purpose and mission of the organization.

Clarity of goals includes the *bottom line* in each workplace, work group, or department; the *work processes* to be improved; and the *human behaviors* (human factor goals) that must change in order to reach those goals. Clarity also includes *major initiatives or projects* that must be successfully accomplished in order to hit the bottom-line goals.

The majority of managers I've met were, unfortunately, closer to the plant manager in scenario 2. In fact, the two scenarios above are based on real people: Plant manager 1 exceeded his goals. Clarity of goals was just one of the reasons he did so, but can you imagine him being successful if he just would have said, "We have to do better"?

The difference between clear goals and no goals is obvious, but the continuum is between no and way-too-many goals. Somewhere in between lies the sweet spot for every business. Although having too many goals is rare, I worked in one business where they told me they have 172 key performance indicators (KPIs). Since there is a wide continuum, art and science are involved in developing workplace goals. The art lies in the ability to find the right goals and the right number of goals on which to focus in order to meet your overall bottom-line objectives. The science lies in the defining and tracking of the goals.

WHAT IS A GOAL?

Developing workplace goals may sound easy, but it is a challenge for many. It is common that people do not know their goals and do not even understand what a goal is. Many create actions or lists of tasks and think they are goals. In fact, the distinction between an action, a standard, and a goal is often confused.

Here is a quick way to think about it, with examples from sales:

An action—Create a service standard for customer requests.
A standard—Reply to customer requests within one hour.
A goal—Reach customer request service standard 95 percent of the time.

Use this analysis to revisit your goals and determine if indeed they are actions or standards. Then sharpen your goals and decide how to best track them.

To improve results, focus on these three goal-related areas: *bottom-line goals*, *work processes*, and *human factors*. Beyond those three major categories, it is common for any workplace to have a certain number of *initiatives* and/or *major projects* that also should be vetted to ensure that they link to the strategic objectives and are properly resourced.

TYPES OF WORKPLACE GOALS

Robert Crosby created the following model with Don Simonic at Alcoa. Simonic saw beyond bottom-line goals to the work processes that needed to be improved in order to reach them. He then went one step further and connected the employees, thus creating human factors (see figure below).

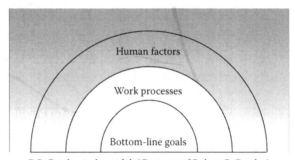

R.P. Crosby goals model. (Courtesy of Robert P. Crosby.)

Bottom-Line Goals

Bottom-line goals are the reason each area, department, or workplace exists (for sales, it is a specific revenue number). Most businesses set goals each year only at the bottom line: X revenue, X safety, X production, X inventory, etc. This may work at a corporate level, but to focus the business on how to actually reach the bottom line, you must include two other categories. The first is work processes (WPs).

Work Processes

Since BLGs are the reason you exist (for sales, it is a specific revenue number), WPs are how the work flows through each area. In other words, WPs are your task *inputs*, *throughputs*, and *outputs*. The category of work processes is critical because identifying the processes that run the business and improving them have a direct impact on the bottom line. In the example used to start this chapter, that same manager started with his bottom-line goal and held sessions where the employees themselves identified and developed which work processes were keeping them from reaching that goal.

Work process improvement requires at least a strategy and perhaps a strategy coupled with a measurable goal. Since some items are harder to measure, such as reducing iterations of reports on quality audits or making sure materials are always on time when there are hundreds of materials on the manufacturing floor, often putting in place a work process improvement strategy is sufficient as long as it is well known and given ample focus to improve. Measure it if you can and create a goal, but if measuring takes too much time and effort, then stay focused on improvement. Clearly, some things still need measurable goals to better understand the problem. Deciding which work processes to improve and whether or not to measure them is where the art of managing comes in.

Focus on work process improvement is key to creating an engaged workplace. All employees know problems with the processes they use on a day-to-day basis to complete their tasks. Engage your employees to improve them and you will change the dynamics within your workplace. Do it consistently and you will win their hearts and minds and, all the while, improve the bottom line.

All areas have work processes, yet most overlook opportunities to drive behavior change by setting specific, measurable goals for the critical processes and then tracking improvement.

Outcome Goals vs. Work Processes

Bottom-line goals are about outcomes: amount of sales, amount of production, on-time shipments are all examples. In contrast, work processes concern *how* processes lead to the outcomes: number of quotes, order accuracy, and hit rate of quotes. Workplaces need a balance of both focus areas. All work groups should know their bottom-line goals and, depending on your organizational position, a few work processes to improve in order to get there.

Human Factors

The final area of focus is human factors (HFs). Businesses are constantly changing. HFs are strategies put in place to engage your employees in workplace improvement: in other words, processes or methods that you use to engage your employees in continuously improving work processes and bottom-line goals. HFs range from problem-solving methods around a specific cross-functional problem, or intact work group development processes. They may include training needs, or role and decision clarity. Engaging employees to solve business problems must not be left up to chance. Keeping up with the human side of business is a performance need that must be worked on year-in and year-out. Stop working on it and you will fall behind. Human factor strategies can also include basic trainings, clarity of help chains, role clarity, and higher-level skills such as effective conflict resolution.

Figuring out how to identify and focus on your bottom-line goals is a challenge worth taking. Once you are clear about goals and strategies, then the actions to improve the workplace become much easier. Until you discover the actual goals you need to achieve in your workplace, based on the real situation you are in, you will be feeling in the dark, hoping that you are doing the right thing.

Do you know which work processes are causing you trouble?

If yes, have you set clear goals for each in order to improve them?

If not, how can you identify them?

Do you know how to involve your employees in significant ways to improve your work processes and bottom line?

If not, how can you learn?

These three categories are in a symbiotic relationship. Human factors should support your work processes. Work processes should directly improve your bottom-line goals. When you engage your employees in the right way, they will be able to improve the work processes. When you reach or exceed the work process goals—assuming you choose the "right" ones—so also will you achieve or exceed your bottom-line goals.

Each area has the potential for dozens of human factors and work processes but, to be effective, you can only choose the number you can tackle with the resources that you have. Business-critical bottom-line goals tend to be easier to identify, whereas work processes and human factors represent the art of managing. But every department and work team has work processes and human factors that must be tracked in order for effective work to be maintained. Each organizational level has a different responsibility to uphold for the business as a whole to succeed. Those in the executive level must do their tasks, working toward their goals, just as those at each level of leadership and work group.

FINITE RESOURCES AND PRIORITIES

All workplaces have a finite number of resources. Some, of course, have more resources than others. Yet resource constraints are a reality all must face. Therefore, goal clarity is key to setting priorities. When you combine clear goals with your major projects and/or initiatives, you find your real resource constraints. Lack of such clarity results in resources working on things that may or may not be mission critical. Once you align to your goals from the top to the bottom of your organization, then you will be able to make informed choices to better address the real needs of your organization.

Alignment to goals takes strong leadership because it requires time, patience, and a lot of communication. Ensuring goal alignment is critical in order to make sure that you are utilizing the finite number of resources you have on the right things. Goals need to be aligned in each intact work group. The process, if done well, will not only clarify priorities but will help your whole organization learn and improve.

It is very dangerous to leave the decision about whether or not to have a conversation to clarify goals up to each work group. Given the choice, many managers would rather just limit their employees' focus to the task at hand. Without such a conversation, employees will not learn about the real priorities, and managers will not learn from their employees about the little things that could make or break reaching these goals. The former is more likely than the latter. Because of these dimensions, some of your employees may be working on things that do not really matter much in the big picture. Additionally, managers who are not educated by their employees may undervalue some small things that make a big difference in the long run, and, inadvertently, lead their employees in a different direction.

IMPORTANCE OF BALANCE

Make sure that the goals you create are balanced and complementary. If you set a goal to increase production, it will not help you much unless you also have a goal to improve or at least maintain quality.

Which Goals Are Appropriate for Which Level?

Since each level of the organization has a different focus, it follows that different types of goals are appropriate for each level. Since those higher in the organization do less process work, it is not necessarily needed to create work process goals at the CEO level.

CEO-Level Goals

Every organization needs a focal point to rally everyone around. Most are not very clear about what is really important; developing a written set of key focus areas and the associated metrics provides this clarity. It also serves to keep people focused over time. By coming back to these critical few things in ongoing reviews and meetings, it serves as a constant reminder about what is truly important. Without this, people will start to substitute their own priorities or, worse yet, become focused on actions and not results.

Brian Bauerbach
CEO, Mold Rite Plastics

Sales	Customer service
Orders booked	Delivery performance as promised
Net sales	Days late to promise date
A/R days sales outstanding	Lead time
Dollars quoted	Customer complaint rate
Value add margin %	Customer claim dollars
Value add dollars	
Financial	**Manufacturing**
Ebita: Earnings before interest, taxes, depreciation, amortization	Conversion cost/1000
	Labor cost/1000
Ebitda % of sales that is profit	Manufacturing cost/1000
SGA: Expense selling, general administration cost	Inventory dollars
	Inventory days
SGA divided by volume of sales	Labor hours worked
Cash for additional debt reduction	Production per labor hour
A/P days to pay	Production volume
Capital spending as % of profit	Maintenance supply spending
People	**Safety**
Employee turnover	OSHA recordable rate
Number of employees	Lost work day rate
Percent overtime	

Example CEO-level goals

The example above is one CEO's list of measures to track. Although the list is not exhaustive, it is a good representation of a manager list to follow and one that gives a broad view. At the CEO and leadership team level of a medium-to-large organization, the view needs to be both broad and holistic. You must look at many facets and make strategic decisions to position your business for success. Hence the large number of things to measure as indicated on the previous page. Note that at the CEO level, there will be a combination of output and process goals, yet they are not tracking the work processes per se.

Additionally, at this level of the organization, you may set broad human factor strategies to increase your employees' ability to engage effectively. If your business culture is struggling and you do not set strategies from the highest level that include yourself and your lead team, then you will leave it up to chance.

Department Goals

Depending on the size of the company you work for, these goals may be much like the CEO-level goals. Yet, if you are a small plant of 200 people or less, your department goals may take on more of a work group feel. You must set clear bottom-line goals, and clear work process and human factor goals and strategies. And you may or may not have specific projects or initiatives.

Work Team Goals

At the work team level, goal setting is quite clear. Set a bottom-line goal, set the right amount of work process goals, and set complementary human factor strategies. HFs and WPs may emerge over time through conversations, or, as it becomes obvious, you must improve a facet of your work group.

How Many Goals Are Appropriate?

Now we are back to the art of managing. As I mentioned earlier: "The difference between clear goals and no goals is obvious, but the continuum is between no and way-too-many goals. Somewhere in between lies the sweet spot for every business. Although having too many goals is rare, I worked in one business where they told me they have 172 key performance indicators (KPIs). Since there is a wide continuum, art and science are involved in developing workplace goals. The art lies in the ability to find the right goals and the right number of goals on which to focus in order to meet your overall bottom-line objectives. The science lies in the defining and tracking of the goals."

All work groups need clear goals, but how many? Which ones are best for each situation? Those questions are best answered by each individual manager. What I can suggest is that you start with one or two bottom-line goals, two or three work process goals, and one or two human factor strategies. The larger your company and the higher you rise, your goals must be broad enough to keep pace with the whole organization.

Goals have a lot of science and some art.

Major Projects and Initiatives

Projects and initiatives are critical to get right. If it is important enough to do, then it is important enough to set clear metrics. All projects must have a *set of specific goals* with the addition of having a *clear timeline* in which they need to be achieved. The simple way of saying it is *what are you trying to achieve* and *by when*?

We will produce a 26 mm bottle cap, at a low weight (clearly specified) by September of this year. We will produce a capping machine for a specific type of bottle, that will run at a higher speed, by February of next year.

Why do you need a completion date? There are a few reasons. One, a completion date forces real conversations about resources. Two, most projects in competitive markets are intended to help get an edge on your competition or fill a gap in your customers' experience; a completion date then is important to maintain or gain business. Finally, the act of setting a completion date is an act of making a commitment. No completion date equals no commitment.

In fact, for major projects or initiatives, there is a definable list of task components to put in place in addition to the goals, at a minimum, to help ensure success. The following graphic represents that list, which is slightly modified from Robert Crosby's book *The Cross-Functional Workplace*.

Write here the project goals, major milestones, and the completion date.	Check task component items not yet effectively in place
_____	☐ Initiating Sponsor (Effectively Sponsoring)
_____	☐ SPA (Project Manager)
_____	☐ Sustaining Sponsors (Effectively Sponsoring)
_____	☐ Decision Matrix
_____	☐ Visual Timeline Posted (SPA, What, By When for each task)
_____	☐ Plans for follow through sessions
_____	☐ Kick-off (To clarify this list to organization)

Goal/task components project work sheet

Note: On this list, I have written "Effectively Sponsoring," since you do not "put" sponsors in place; they already exist. Most miss this critical distinction. The task is to align and build sponsorship once you identify who the actual sponsors are. The sponsor of the work may or may not be sponsoring it effectively.

Software Development Goals

Director of engineering: "I want you to know that with the resources we have and the requirements and quality that you are asking for, I can complete this project by October of next year."

Senior manager: "What? We need it done by February!"

Director of engineering: "OK, get me more resources and I can do it, or change some of the requirements."

Senior manager: "But the requirements are set."

Director of engineering: "Hmm. Well, that only leaves resources?"

Senior manager: "Wow. No one has ever talked to me about these dynamics before."

Director of engineering: "Really? How often have you delivered your products on time and to the right specs?"

Senior manager: "Well … actually, we are always late and often missing some key parts."

Director of engineering: "I was beginning to guess that. Look, I want to be honest and deliver what I say, when I say I will."

Senior manager: "That sounds great, but difficult."

Software projects can miss their mark for many reasons. First, the alignment issues dealt with throughout this book happen in all types of workplaces; lack of clarity of priorities and goals is commonplace. As you will see later in my chapter on Sponsor, Agent, Target, Advocate (SATA) workplace examples, many large initiatives are running in software firms that are not very well aligned. Second, since software is a virtual world, defining the requirements becomes even more critical. In a virtual world, whatever you can imagine you can do; so, if you do not set limits, you may lose control fast. Finally, unrealistic resourcing based on the first two leaves many thinking they will meet deadlines not well thought out.

The following is a software model intended to help you determine the real needs of any given project.

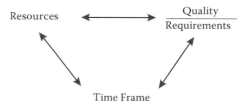

Triangle model. (Courtesy of Chris Crosby.)

Time Frame

The time frame is self-explanatory. It is simply the date on which you want to ship the software product. In other words, when you want the project done.

Quality and Requirements

Several interrelated issues follow:

Quality
In the software industry, this is about how well you debug the system. Quality here is about how much risk there is of the product crashing or a feature not working correctly.

Level 1. A website. If a website crashes, very little damage will be done unless it is the primary means of doing business. My company's website could crash, yet it would cause very little damage to our business. In contrast, if Amazon's website crashed for an extended period of time, they would suffer a huge economic blow.

Level 2. Software to run a business: commonly called an ERP system, yet it could be any variety of systems necessary for organizational functioning. If this system goes down, it could cost a large company a lot of money. It could be hundreds of thousands or even millions.

Level 3. A defibrillator. If the software used to run a defibrillator crashes, someone might die.

To a great degree, the quality of your product should depend on how well it solves customer needs.

Requirements
These are the software specifications guiding the engineers' efforts. The more complex the requirements are, the longer it takes to create and effectively debug the software.

Resources

All development firms have a finite number of resources. Their availability and efficiency dictate the speed at which you can create your software.

The triangle model is intended to help plan effectively by pointing out the levers that exist within a software development project. Once you set any of the points on the triangle model, you narrow your options for affecting the project. For example, if the ship date is set (time frame), you only have features/quality or resources that a manager can use as levers to achieve your business goals. A common misconception is to believe that you can keep all three points of the triangle unchanged and yet inspire or encourage your work group to correct a slipping "ship" date or missed milestones.

Project corrections require a return to goal setting with a pragmatic look at the three options articulated in the triangle model. If you want to keep the same requirements and quality standards, then your lever is to add resources. Most high-level managers, in any business, hate that solution. The problem is that if you do not add resources, reduce quality, or simplify requirements, you will extend your timeline. *This book is about such conversations*, and then making real sacrifices to get the product completed on time and with the appropriate level of quality so your customers are fully satisfied. The conversation at the beginning of this chapter was the beginning of an honest discussion about actual constraints facing the business. In contrast, an unaware workplace *will not* have the difficult conversations, will keep working onward, and will keep missing deadlines.

The software industry has moved to different models which play with requirements and quality as well as with ship dates. From *Waterfall* to *Agile* (originally called *Spiral*) to an integrated model that involves things called *Tribes, Squads, Chapters,* and *Guilds,* all are methods attempting to solve the triangle in new ways. Subscription services incorporate this because the product gets multiple updates; therefore, products "ship" much more frequently than in the past: from yearly, to monthly, to weekly, and, when trying to fix multiple bugs, sometimes daily.

ALIGNING PROJECTS AND INITIATIVES

Most workplaces have an abundance of ideas and potential improvements that employees want to work on. If you are not careful, the number of extra initiatives will get out of control, to the point where nobody has any extra time and many initiatives are not getting completed. The best managers understand this and have a way of both tracking the extra initiatives as well as managing them. By "managing them" I mean having the right conversations to determine what should be done now and what can be delayed or stopped altogether. The vetting process in determining what projects or initiatives to work on should include circling back to your bottom-line goals to ensure you are working on the items that will help your current situation and position yourself in the marketplace.

In one situation, a business I worked with listed all their projects and initiatives. It turned out they had 38 initiatives and key projects that were taxing their resources, many of which they were unaware. The leaders then worked a process to talk about and clarify each, reducing the number to fewer than 20, only keeping those deemed "mission critical" to their goals.

High-level leaders beware! Due to your organizational position, when you wander the halls people may think that your thoughts are suggestions and start working on them. This is not a call to stay in your office. Leaders must stay in touch with their work force, yet it is a call to be aware of this dynamic and take precautions to make sure you send a clear message.

A note about initiatives—be careful when creating initiatives that you are clear about what problem you are trying to solve. Many create solutions or sets of actions that are hard to quantify because they did not exercise due diligence as to what problem they are trying to solve. The problem statement reads as an action or standard and there is no quantifiable goal. Therefore, they act and say that they have completed a project or initiative, yet they may have not really solved anything.

Go back to the third page of this chapter and check to see if your initiative is a clear goal. Is it an action, a standard, or a work process goal? If so, then what problem are you trying to solve at a higher level? Take any work process goal and get it as close to a bottom-line goal as possible, if appropriate. Problem-solving goals, like for lean's Kaizen events, may remain at the work process level. One example coming from the manufacturing world is changeovers. The goal is to reduce the time to move from producing different colors or different products in half. The clearer you are about what problem you are trying to solve, the easier it will be to gain organization alignment to solve it.

IMPORTANCE OF UNDERSTANDING "THE BIG PICTURE"

"The Big Picture" is the larger situation you face in the marketplace: the current market conditions, how effectively your organization is doing in that market, and, most importantly, what areas you must improve in order to gain a better market position. Do you understand where your business stands in relationship to its competitors? Most employees do not, yet that very information is often driving decisions at the top that impact the employees at all levels.

I am often surprised, in difficult moments, how rare it is that workplaces share the actual situations they face. Instead, they tend to try top-down, short-sighted emergency measures that demoralize the employees and mostly fail because they are conducted too far from the people who really know the possible solutions that would work much better. Kurt Lewin, talking about the WWII war with Japan, stated:

In such a situation no special effort is required to keep morale high. The very combination of a definitive objective, the belief in final success and the realistic facing of great difficulties is high morale. The individual who makes extreme efforts and accepts great risks for worthwhile goals does not feel that he is making a sacrifice, instead he merely feels that he is acting naturally. (Lewin, 1997)

OK, so most companies are not fighting a war, yet in today's workplace, there are many dire scenarios of which the employees are unaware; the leaders have not shared the real pain they are in. How many plants have you heard about which were suddenly closed and moved to a new location in order to produce the product more cheaply? Imagine how hard the workers would work if they knew the scenario they were in and the production improvements they needed to achieve to keep the plant in place. Add in the mix solid problem-solving and workplace improvement strategies and likelihood of success gets even greater.

In dire circumstances, just sharing the situation is not enough. You need to also have a plan, complete with a solid structure, and process to involve employees in helping solve the issues. To do that, you need the organization alignment this book advocates. With such a strategy, you can involve those closest to the work, and not only reach unthinkable business numbers but also increase morale along the way. Cost cutting and increasing production are a few of the areas that can most easily be achieved with a combination of honesty and an effective people strategy to solve the problems.

On the flip side, I have seen business after business solve their yearly cost problems or production issues by making decisions from on high and imposing them below. In each scenario, businesses who maintained the pattern each year slowly self-destructed into layoffs, early retirements, and significant loss of market share.

TRACKING AS A FORM OF LISTENING

I have found that the act of tracking items and setting goals around that tracking is a deep form of listening. Most think they don't have the time to do so. Yet, if you spend the time to listen by tracking what is going on, you will save a lot of time.

John Nicol
Partner and General Manager, Microsoft

I have worked with many people who said they were having problems and were not actually tracking the areas where they were struggling. In most of those cases, just by tracking the items they were concerned with the obvious problems emerged and the organizations were able to solve their issues.

John Nicol talked about taking over a division that had developed set-top boxes providing consumers with Internet access. On hearing reports that customers were upset by lack of service, he was unclear of the cause or extent of the problem. His first act was to track all devices by pinging them, then noting their location on a US map. He prominently positioned a large LCD monitor, so the engineers could see the real-time problem and track progress. The first thing they learned was that a whole area of the southeast had poor service or even no service. The very act of tracking gave them data to confirm the magnitude of the issue; from there they put in place measures that ensured all customers were online.

In a similar experience at a print shop having problems with late shipments, I asked: "How many are late?" The manager replied: "I am not sure." So, I asked him to start tracking each job and recording each late shipment and its cause(s). He did so by using a large whiteboard and displaying it prominently to visually track all the print jobs so that all the employees could easily see them. This simple act of tracking and providing a feedback loop to the workplace quickly led to discovering little issues that were solvable, and within a few weeks they had reduced the late shipments to less than 5 percent of all orders. Not all situations are quite so simple, yet surely there are many where simple tracking can aid learning and quick workplace improvements.

GOAL ALIGNMENT

Setting goals can add excitement and challenge to your workplace. For many, however, it is just another mundane task. Once you use your goals to align your workplace, they will take on new meaning and energy. I started this chapter by saying, "The fundamental task of leadership is to align their employees in the same direction. Workplace goals represent that direction." Therefore, just setting clear goals is not enough. You must use those goals to *align* and *engage* your work force in order to translate the direction to results! Since there are finite resources in all workplaces, aligning them to successfully reach your goals represents a challenge that is worthy of engaging all employees to help solve. Don't miss this opportunity.

Most businesses treat goal setting as an annual event, yet miss the golden opportunity it presents. The most common practice is to set next year's goals X percent higher than last and then move on to "real work," no matter how clear or fuzzy the plan. Normally the pressure to "get to work" far outweighs the pressure to "plan and reflect on the work." The opportunity missed is to not only align the employees to the goals, but also to engage them in creating a plan on how to reach them. Engage and align effectively and you create a far greater chance of success. After such an effort, if the business falls short, it is likely because of factors outside of its control—like a global recession!—however, major improvements on indexes of cost, quality, productivity, and safety will still be obtained.

Effective goal alignment has some key components and requires time spent "planning the work" despite pressure to get going. It is also an iterative process in which each business can only start wherever they are and move toward clarity. Skip this and the likelihood of incremental sustainable improvements decreases.

Once you have created clear goals, as outlined in this chapter, you are ready for the next steps in the process. Here are the key components.

Use an effective group process and cascade to all major groups— Alignment of goals requires engaging all employees who work to achieve them. That alignment must be done in intact work groups. Clarity and retention are increased through dialogue, a constructive back-and-forth on a topic, rather than through one-way communication. Remember, psychologists say people only retain 30 percent of what they read. Most finish a book only if engaged, yet even then only retain around 30 percent.

Despite this, many give goals through one-way communication, which contributes to a passive workplace. Use of an effective group process that involves dialogue, and critical thinking in each intact work group is a key component of successful goal alignment.

Most managers are deficient here. At best, they have read about group process but have little or no formal training. At worst, they were trained in a technical field, excelled in their craft, and are now responsible to manage people and lead groups.

To cascade goal alignment, start with the lead team. Have the manager clarify the corporate goals, share them with the rest of the lead team, and create the location or division's goals. Roll the division goals back up to the corporate manager to verify that they are the right goals to reach the corporate objectives. From here, the task is to dialogue about the goals and have the group suggest work processes that need more focus.

Once that conversation is complete, it is time to dive deeper into the organization. Think of the overall goals as a large pie with each department responsible for their piece. Have all department heads develop their piece that supports the division's goals in all three categories. (Often, I also have them generate feedback on what they need from the other departments in order to reach their goals.) After that, each department head presents its goals (and feedback) to the whole lead team, and then works the data through a dialogue. The top manager must say whether the department is on the right track, with help from the rest of the group, and adjust what each department is working on, if needed, in order to make sure they are working on the right things to reach the overall goals. Through this process, the lead team will create greater clarity on the goals they are working on, a greater understanding of what all departments are trying to achieve, and what they need from each other to get there. Each department should create approximately 1 to 2 BLGs, 3 to 5 WPs, and 1 to 2 HFs (although there is no magic number).

Next, work with each department and each intact work team to clarify the goals, and have the employees raise the critical issues needed to reach them. Go as far down the organization as you can, remembering that hourly employees are very knowledgeable about the best way to achieve results. Warning! Bosses must still decide on priorities and follow up robustly. Failure to follow up could have the unintended consequence of slighting those who have given ideas. If you do not follow up well, do not blame the employees for being skeptical the next time you ask for input.

Connecting task to big picture—If done well, all employees should understand how their task fits into their department's goals, how those, in turn, fit into the division or location's and, ultimately, the corporation's goals. *Imagine the power of having all your employees understand how their tasks help the business reach its overall goals!*

See across the whole system—here are a few things to look for.

Victim thinking—For example, "I have always gotten bad information from X (any department); that is just the way it is." It is easy to get used to the status quo, and departments often get stuck in their silos. It does not have to be that way, however. Strategies can be created to solve problems of missing data from any department and begin to reduce errors. Each person who does not take appropriate responsibility for accurate inputs and information is helping to maintain the status quo.

Work process goals out of whack—There is a tendency for each department to focus on the bad or missing stuff from every other department and to not put appropriate WPs in place, needed to drive improvements from their own employees. This is really another form of victim thinking. If a facilitator listens to the problems of each group, obvious gaps in focus will appear; these need to be addressed. Sales may forget to take steps to reduce order errors, production may forget to focus on critical process errors, and engineering may forget to focus on Bill of Materials accuracy. The goal is to have each intact group and department take full responsibility for their own areas, as well as understand the interconnectedness of the workplace.

Follow this with a session where all department managers gather to further see across the whole system. In this session, share learnings, derive implications, and build further strategies for improvement.

Be diligent—It is easy to let a people process get away from you. A process like this will allow you to learn and understand all the issues in your workplace. It is easy to leave with a huge laundry list and only accomplish some of it. Finish off the first go-round with honest conversations about how much work the list really requires and what you will and will not work on based on your current resource realities, needs, and priorities. The lead team must make decisions and justify, through both financial numbers and potential morale implications to their workforce, what to work on. This becomes even more critical if it is obvious that the list got larger than available resources can achieve. Part of the decision process has to be to notice items that seem little, but that can make or break what gets done.

This is the work and responsibility of the lead team. Refining what will be worked on is best done in dialogue with the location manager and the rest of the staff. Stretch yourself but also be realistic. Ultimately, your department may have to work on some things that you do not deem important. Equally important is communicating with your group about which items get taken off the list and why. Most employees can live with decisions that they disagree with, if they at least understand why.

Finally, you must follow up this work. Within a few months, spend the time to bring all groups back together to take a look and make course corrections. Leaving goal alignment up to checking off a list at the end of the year misses the mark. Remember the pressure to "get to work" far outweighs the pressure to "plan the work" in most organizations. Do not let that stop you from having people pause for a few hours and continue planning the work. The follow-up must go beyond "did you do the task" to dialogue about whether you are getting the intended results. After all, these tasks were just the best guess at what would solve the problem. Even if they were done well, the problem may not be solved. The cost of not doing follow-up, in both real dollars and organizational momentum, is too great to let it slide. Goal alignment gives every business a golden opportunity. Seize it with an effective group process and create a clear and unified path toward business results!

Once you clarify your goals, then your employees will have tangible items around which to align. The next step of organization alignment is a theory that is perhaps the most critical in order to do this, called "Sponsor Agent Target Advocate." You were introduced to this model towards the end of Chapter 10 in this book. *Strategic Organizational Alignment*, by Chris Crosby, applies that model in much more depth.

12

Decision Making

In my father's first organization development book, *Walking the Empowerment Tightrope: Balancing Management Authority & Employee Influence*, he identified 25 high-performance factors (based on a survey used in thousands of organizations), which, if in place, resulted in and reflected a high-performance work culture. The following three factors in particular are a huge variable in creating that culture:

Factor 4. *Distinguish between decision making and influence*: Managers are clear about the distinction between "who is deciding" versus "who is influencing" and communicate that.

Factor 5. *Decisions are made*: Decisions are made in an expedient amount of time; it does not take forever to get a decision made.

Factor 6. *Implementation*: Once decisions are made, they are effectively implemented in a timely way.

Decision making is a deceptively simple cultural factor in organizational and project success, one often taken for granted or misunderstood ("single point accountability for decisions…you mean I can decide whatever I want?"). Lack of decision-making clarity is an insipid cause of waste. The graph in Figure 12.1, adapted from Tannenbaum and Schmidt, provides guidance toward a thoughtful and effective approach.

High productivity behaviors: Relentlessly eliminate confusion by clarifying single point accountability for all tasks and decisions. Lean heavily on consultative and delegative styles, with effective dialogue/input prior to decisions. Constantly seek clarity regarding who will decide what, how, and by when. The two middle styles are the most reliable and engaging styles, although all four are necessary for effective leadership.

Decide and Tell:	Consultative:	Delegation:	Group decisions (Vote or Consensus):
Leader decides without input—this authority is vital for certain functions and situations, but should not be overused.	Leader is pretty certain about what to decide but wants input first, or is uncertain about what to do and wants input—either way leader will make the decision after hearing from others. Ideal decision-making style in that it balances clarity about who decides with participation/input.	Leader delegates the decision to another individual, with clear parameters, and eliminates waste by allowing decisions to be made as close to the action as possible.	Often promoted because of values and with good intentions, but usually inefficient and/or poorly managed, resulting in "tyranny" of majority or of most influential.

FIGURE 12.1
Decision styles. (Based on the work of Tannenbaum and Schmidt.)

Decision clarity tips: Decision clarity is essential during change as well as during everyday work. Time and again I've witnessed bosses who say "we need to decide this" in a meeting, as if using a consensus style of decision making, when they know full well that if the group doesn't voice a decision to their liking, they will make the call. The problem in these situations is not that the boss is going to decide, but that they are really using a consultative process and calling it something else. The effect is mixed at best: sometimes harmless, often confusing, and potentially demoralizing if subordinates begin to suspect their involvement in decisions is just a trick.

In the nuclear industry, this was referred to as "bring me a rock." If repeated often enough, the subordinates may avoid voicing true alternatives for fear of being overruled anyway (which can also be a subtle form of public humiliation, whether intended or not). Worse, they will likely repeat the leader's behavior with their own subordinates, and so on and so forth down the chain of command. It's essentially an attempt at avoiding the conflict that can easily arise with difficult decisions, by pretending that everyone has equal input and praying that for the most part everyone will agree. Even worse is when a team is formed to "come up with a solution," works on their solution for months thinking that they are deciding, only to have it rejected in the end. Such sloppy "engagement" around decision making creates needless confusion and drama.

Subordinates consistently respect a boss who says, "I need to make this decision…I want to hear your views first," and then does a good job of exploring the available opinions, rather than debating them away. Again, paraphrasing (described in Appendix A) is a critical skill if you want to genuinely understand the ideas/perspectives of others. Armed with true understanding, the boss is then in the best possible position to make the call. And who wouldn't want to be armed with the best possible information prior to making a tough decision?

Then comes the moment of truth. If it's truly a tough call, with potential consequences for the organization, with possible competing and clashing alternatives, then some are going to like it and others are not. That is the territory of a decision-making role. It can't be avoided by saying "we all decide," if that is not what you really mean. Clarity about who, how, and when to make the decision eliminates needless conflict about how the decision will be made. Decision clarity streamlines the process (which is of necessity a process repeated daily throughout the organization on decisions big and small), allowing you to concentrate instead on coming together to implement once a decision is made. Subordinates will feel respected if their views were really solicited and explored prior to the decision, versus feeling resentful and second-guessing if the decision was made without full knowledge of their own pertinent information.

For all of the reasons mentioned, decision clarity is a huge and practical cultural factor in high performance. If done well, the result is engagement, decisions made on the best possible information, and speed. People are sometimes surprised by this last point, thinking that if they really listen, it will slow things down. Effective listening is not the time killer. Confusion, second-guessing, and waffling are what slow things down. Decision making in a nuclear power plant control room during any sort of crisis is a good example. The decision is single point (the shift manager) and if done well, truly consultative. In a matter of minutes, the shift manager briefs the control room operators, carefully checks with each to see if they have additional information, and decides on a course of action. If there is confusion about decision-making authority in the control room, as occurred in the Clinton Nuclear Generating Station Significant Event Report (a VP's presence in the control room in a culture that wasn't crystal clear on decision-making authority resulted in ambiguity about who was in charge during an event), then the process breaks down. Fortunately that is a very rare occurrence in that industry!

The Clinton event illustrates another critical cultural factor. Decision clarity is not and should not be automatically determined by hierarchical position. In one organization after another, when I ask people to tell me who makes a certain decision, the kneejerk answer is the top of the hierarchy. Often people will answer "the CEO" when referring to daily operational decisions! This of course is rarely accurate, thank goodness, as everyone, including the janitor, is making decisions about how to manage their time and do their job.

This is as it should be, but it should be explicit between each boss and their subordinates, not seemly stumbled into. In other words, the boss should decide who decides and what style they should use, while pushing the decision making as close to the action as possible. It is needless waste, and disempowering, if a worker has adequate information to make a call, but has to wait on the boss, or go find them, simply because of a poor use of the structure of hierarchy. During my work in one aluminum fabrication plant, the workers at high speed tables processing aluminum into desired shapes had to go find the boss if the process started to go out of control. They weren't authorized to push the big red "stop" buttons on the side of the tables! If a boss happened to be there, they would yell "Stop!" without thinking. But in the absence of the boss, scrape would pile everywhere, and production would suffer major delays. I remember how embarrassed the workers and the supervisors were when this issue surfaced. Sometime in their past history, there had been fear that workers would stop the process for the wrong reasons. This fear certainly insulted the pride of the current operators. This was a good example of making a rule for everyone to manage one person's behavior or potential behavior, a demoralizing mistake I have seen many companies make. Of course, in this example, the leadership immediately delegated that authority to the operators. After a brief trial period, it became their standard decision-making procedure at the tables.

Most opportunities for delegation aren't that obvious. But there are still many in almost every organization. Don't let your habits around trust (as explored in Chapter 7) lead you to either underdelegate or overdelegate. Delegation is a critical skill, attempted by many but mastered by few. The following guide to delegation is excerpted from my father's book, *Cultural Change in Organizations*:

> Delegation is obviously not new. However, there are some traps that frequently derail its effectiveness. The most common is to delegate without clear boundaries and/or expectations about how to monitor the work. Out of sight and mind does not mean a lack of accountability. The questions below are intended to help you appropriately delegate authority in order to create a faster and more effective organization. They provide a methodical way to put in appropriate checks and balances. Delegation without due

diligence to these questions is more accurately called abdication and could lead to lack of clarity, poor results, and no quality control.

1. What is the task or new decision accountability?
2. Is the employee ready now or do you need to get them ready?
   - If no, what training do they need?
3. What are the parameters?
   - Within what boundaries can they operate?
4. If things go wrong what are they to do?
   - When do they call you for help?
   - When and under what conditions are they to call any resource for help?
5. Do they know how it fits into the greater system?
   - If no, explain how it fits.
6. How will it be monitored?
   - The intention of this stage is to have a dialogue between you and your employee to develop a monitoring system that (a) provides the information that you need and (b) is simple. How often you are updated is based on the experience of your worker.

(Used with permission from Robert P. Crosby.)

Delegation is both art and science. Choosing what and when to delegate is the art. Gaining specificity on the task components and the monitoring system is the science. The responsibility to monitor the work is yours. However, the responsibility to keep you informed is the employees'. Therefore, the employee should be involved in developing the monitoring system. An effective strategy is to have them develop the system and share it with you for approval. The aim is to create a system that is easy for the employee and provides you with the required information.

Delegation is a process, not an end state. If used well, you will create a workplace that moves fast, significantly engages its employees, and reaches or exceeds its bottom-line goals. The paradox of delegation is that in order to gain control, you must push some decision-making authority closer to your employees. The process outlined here is intended to help you do that in a methodical way that avoids the extreme of delegation which is abdication. Without effective monitoring of the delegated work, you risk losing touch with your workers and having them inadvertently move the business in a direction that ultimately could hurt the bottom line.

Again, as mentioned by my father, delegation, and the quest for decision-making clarity, is a process, not an end state. As leaders and subordinates come and go, as technology changes, and so on, the organization must constantly look at and clarify who decides what, how, and by when (of equal importance, and no business conversation should end without it, is who will *do* what, and by when). Create decision clarity via a matrix or similar process (see table below). Identify key decision points in daily operations and key change initiatives. Especially be alert based on prior decisions that went poorly, were in conflict, or were exceedingly slow to be made. Use your matrix to clarify who will make what decisions and how, to establish participative decision making, and to surface unresolved issues about authority. Make sure someone with adequate authority has single point accountability for raising a red flag if the decision process you have agreed upon is in some way compromised:

Decision Clarity

Work Issues Requiring Decision	Who Decides	Who's Consulted Prior to Decision	Who Carries Out the Action	Who Needs to Be Informed
1.				
2.				
3.				
4.				

Source: Courtesy of Robert P. Crosby.

Working toward decision clarity is a culture change unto itself, and a good example of the human factor goals mentioned in Chapters 2 and 11. Finally, once you have clarity, emotional intelligence comes back into play as a vital element in organization performance. In Daniel Goleman's latest book, *The Brain and Emotional Intelligence: New Insights*, the latest research reinforces the following—that we can't make a decision without emotion. As important as rational thinking is, our feelings about the different options are key to making choices. Antonio Damasio's research on the brain and emotional intelligence demonstrates that when there is a disconnect between our rational and emotional brains, we can no longer function effectively in our daily lives.

Another compelling finding in Damasio's research is that the basal ganglia, an area deep in the brain and intimately related to the hippocampus, stores our experiences about how previous decisions worked out for us. The basal ganglia is connected to our thinking brain (neocortex) but also connected with our gastrointestinal tract. So when we feel uneasy about a decision, Damasio's findings suggest the validity of "trusting our gut" as one critical component to making a decision.

In other words, make sure the right person is making the call, and that the organization has clarity so that they can implement that person's decision. Then, if you are that person, gather the best information and input you can (in a timely manner), and be rational by respecting your feelings/ gut. Then give yourself and others a break. Not every decision will lead to the desired results. If there was a guarantee, then it would be a "no-brainer." Learn and allow others to learn when things go awry. Keep your batting average up, and you and the organization will succeed. Take a consistent stand by insisting on clarity. Take clear stands and stay connected by creating a sound and engaging process, and then let the designated decision makers make the call.

13

Feedback, Reinforcement, and Reprimand

As leader/manager, part of the decision-making process you must own, absolutely in terms of your direct reports, and by setting the standard of the rest of the organization beneath you, is the selection and evaluation of the people you have in place.

In his best seller, *Good to Great*, Jim Collins wrote that great leaders "start by *getting the right people on the bus*, the wrong people off the bus, and the right people in the right seats" (Collins, 2001). Although catchy, this is a decidedly nonsystemic way of thinking. Of course you want to pick the best people you can. However, how you lead the people you've got is far more important. I've been with many leaders as they take struggling individuals, teams, and entire organizations to higher performance. The biggest variable isn't who is on the bus; the biggest variable is how the bus is being driven, the variable you are working on in this book. Otherwise, how could a low-performing organization quickly become a high-performing organization? I've also seen the opposite far too many times: a high-performing business unit or location begins to struggle after a change in leadership.

Pick the best people you can, of course. I think including their future peers and even subordinates in the selection process is a wise practice. Then lead, and as part of that leadership continuously improve yourself and your people through effective feedback.

Thinking and leading systemically requires giving and receiving feedback at the individual and group level. This is true whether the feedback is given formally or informally. Informal feedback is powerful, free, and grossly underdone behavior. Virtually every employee survey since the beginning of time has conveyed the message that "I only hear what I have done wrong, not what I have done right," and that the primary variable in employee turnover is soured relations with one's boss (which can be prevented by ongoing, effective dialogue). Depending on the study, research on how couples communicate in marriage indicates that marriages last when there is an average of five to seven compliments for every one criticism. While similar research hasn't been replicated in organizations to my knowledge, this isn't a bad standard to adhere to. Compliments ("Thanks for getting that done!") can be delivered in seconds, reinforce desired behavior, and, when genuine, help build connection. A consistent history of appreciation also sets the tone needed for a positive outcome in moments of criticism. This is not, however, the same thing as the misguided advice that one should begin with a compliment when criticizing. I strongly recommend separating the two behaviors. If your compliments are followed by criticisms, the compliments will be disregarded as a gimmick, and increase mistrust in the relationship. Instead, "catch them doing something right" on a regular basis, and handle corrections separately and only as genuinely needed to improve performance.

Whether a compliment or a criticism, Blanchard's "One Minute Manager" model conveys the right idea:

1. Let people know as close to the actual event as possible.
2. Be behaviorally specific (This is critical! Read Appendix A to sharpen your clarity on this skill!)
3. Let them know how you feel ("I love it when…" or "I'm frustrated by…").

To this I would add, be clear and concise and stay connected while the employee processes the information (especially when criticizing!).

Any form of reprimand is an emotional situation, and if you rush the interaction, the odds are high for misunderstanding. The value is lost if the employee doesn't precisely understand the behavior, and exits the interaction thinking "the real problem here is you." In my experience, this happens more often than not, and can only be prevented by patiently getting verbal confirmation of understanding, and listening to the employee's perspective on the behavior/situation you are challenging. You may learn something about the situation that changes your own perspective. Perhaps you even own a piece of what went wrong. But even if the reprimand stands, as at times it should, it is far better if it stands on mutual understanding. If the receiver doesn't have clarity, they are unlikely to succeed in altering their behavior. If they do have clarity and they repeat the behavior, then you have a solid ground for performance management.

Reprimanding is such an emotional process that the assistance of a neutral third party (a facilitator) is often wise.

All of the above can be handled informally (although it is prudent to document reprimands, in case you do head for a termination of the relationship). Formal systems, while certainly in vogue, are replete with unintended side effects and waste. As quality guru Dr. W. Edwards Deming put it in his last interview:

> Appraisal of people is ruinous. You cause humiliation, crush out joy of learning, innovation, joy on the job. Most of what anybody does is governed by the system that he works in. You are not evaluating him, you are evaluating the interaction with him and the system, the rules and constraints he works in. Reward for good performance may be the same as reward to the weatherman for having a nice day. (*Industry Week*, January 17, 1994)

Despite these words, performance appraisal as a standard of managing rolls on. I don't imagine that this annual and semiannual exercise will change, although I'm unaware of any studies that prove it adds value (and I keep searching). Some approaches, however, are better than others. While at PECO Nuclear, a substantial portion of my merit reward was tied to the overall performance of the power plant I served. To me, that makes sense, aligning everyone in the system toward those larger goals, so that no part of the system is tempted to hit their targets even if they are hurting the performance of other parts of the system (controlling inventory costs by starving the plant of needed spare parts is just one possible example of behavior based on department or workgroup goals that deters the overall performance of a system). In the same system, however, individual performance within each group was rated on a bell-shaped curve. That is, even though we were meeting or exceeding the highest industry performance at our power plant, only a small percentage could be assessed as "high performers." The majority were given the middle rating (which no matter how hard management tried to put a rosier image on, it was understood to be "average" and an insult), and a certain percentage had to be given the lowest ranking. If you truly had a team of high performers, it didn't matter, and if you truly were part of a high-performing organization, it still didn't matter. It was an annual, painful, and time-consuming exercise in demoralization, from which the organization had to continually recover.

So if you are using a bell-shaped curve, kill it. You could even save your company a lot of time and money by throwing out the annual appraisal process. Most bosses and subordinates dread the process, and there is wide variation in how it is conducted even within companies. Worse, many bosses don't give feedback until it is annual performance appraisal time. Give timely reinforcement and reprimand (if needed) instead. Work on succession and development plans but don't tie assessment of individuals to pay. Reward based on systemic performance and cost of living increases as systemic performance allows. If you can't influence your appraisal system, or if you don't agree with me about the flaws of such systems, then at least make it the best it can be by giving timely, behaviorally specific feedback to your subordinates, peers, and boss, and seeking the same in return.

Another flawed approach to feedback is to make it anonymous. Every organization I am familiar with in the United States and abroad conducts 360 anonymous feedback surveys for people in leadership positions (90% of all companies, according to an ETS 2012 study). This holds true despite data indicating lack of results and other problems. Here are just two examples:

Watson Wyatt's 2001 Human Capital Index, an ongoing study of the linkages between HR practices and shareholder value at 750 publicly traded US companies, found that companies that use peer review have a market value that is 4.9 percent lower than similarly situated companies that don't use peer review. Companies that allow employees to evaluate their managers are valued 5.7 percent lower than similar firms that don't.

A 2005 meta-analysis of 26 longitudinal studies indicated that it is unrealistic to expect large performance improvement after people receive 360-degree feedback.

Despite such feedback, the use of 360s continues to be widely accepted. All of the research I've read comes to a similar conclusion: The answer is not to scrap them, but rather to improve on how the organization supports learning from the results. It should be noted, however, that all of the research I could find came from companies that sell 360s. Despite the problems indicated by their research, every source remained a proponent of the method.

None of the articles, however, addressed these three fundamental problems:

1. *Anonymous data and feedback leaves recipients and experts alike guessing at the true meaning.*

   The separation of those who provide the data from the task of understanding the data violates a fundamental principle once held dearly by the social science founders of survey feedback. As Ronald Lippitt, who was a close associate of Rensis Likert (the creator of the Likert scale, used in all surveys), put it in a conversation with my father, "They who put their pencil to the survey paper should also see and work the data." This principle has been lost in most survey processes including 360s.

2. *There is a widespread knowledge gap regarding specificity versus judgments in behavioral feedback.*

Behavioral specificity is a concept that many are unfamiliar with and/or is underused (be sure to learn more about this skill by reading Appendix A!). Specificity in feedback sticks strictly with observable behaviors ("when you said or did ____"). Ownership, in this case, means taking personal responsibility for how one takes and interprets what someone else did or said (for example, "when you said or did ____, I was concerned that you might be losing faith in me"). In that example, the speaker started with behavior description ("When you said or did ____"), added a feeling description ("I was concerned"), and finished by admitting their interpretation. Such interpretations ("losing faith" in the last example) come out of our own personal history (I might worry that people will lose faith in me, and project it onto the behavior of others, whereas you might not carry that worry at all). Blame-laden generalizations ("You aren't a team player" or "You're a micromanager") are generally delivered without ownership (i.e., as if they are just a fact about the other) and almost certainly result in defensiveness on the part of the receiver. There is a high likelihood that the receiver will reject such feedback, and even silently blame the giver ("The actual problem here is you"). The predictable result is further erosion of the work relationship, adding to a spiral of even greater fear of giving and receiving feedback. This, in turn, can become the work culture of the organization. In contrast, a high standard of specificity and ownership is much more likely to build strong work relationships and higher organizational performance. It's difficult to hold feedback gathered anonymously to the same standard of specificity and ownership. Consequently, critical comments written anonymously are too often full of generalizations and blame, and thus difficult to truly understand and to receive non-defensively.

3. *There is also a knowledge gap regarding first- and second-order change.*

First-order change is immediate and specific, such as a behavioral change following effective feedback. Second-order change is cultural, such as the impact of how the feedback was gathered and delivered.

Anonymous feedback can inadvertently create negative, second-order change, by reinforcing the fear and avoidance of open, face-to-face feedback. A typical belief in such a culture is that "our people won't be honest unless it is anonymous" and a predictable consequence is that the organization becomes more dependent on experts (whether internal or external) to manage feedback and/or conflict. In contrast, sufficiently skillful direct feedback has the positive second-order effect of creating a culture where people are increasingly willing to have potentially difficult yet much needed work-related conversations. Although upfront training and facilitation is likely needed, the organization becomes less dependent in the long run.

Additional negative effects of anonymous feedback based on the three factors above include the following:

- Because of the low standards of specificity and ownership, the odds of anonymous feedback adding blame-laden generalizations to your permanent employee file are high, thus adding to the fear of the process.
- Even when the 360 is mostly positive, and even when the receiver of the feedback is a competent and mature adult, it is tempting to speculate on who may have offered any "negative" comments, and to hold some resentment against them.
- Without dialogue, the receiver is left guessing at the real meaning of even the most specific comments, hence decreasing the likelihood that the intended lesson will actually get learned.
- By reinforcing anonymity and indirectness, anonymous feedback works against the skillful feedback that is the foundation of high-performance culture, and runs counter to wise corporate values such as openness, trust, and accountability.

WHAT TO DO ABOUT IT

Here are some tips corresponding to the three fundamental problems (above):

1. Use live feedback processes. When surveys are used, which I encourage, of course they should be filled out anonymously. That is not the problem. The potential for individual and organizational

performance improvement lies, however, in allowing the people who filled out the survey to interpret the data, engage in dialogue about how to maintain strengths, and address issues. Rather than an individual guessing at what others meant, or an expert assisting in deriving implications, the recipient gets live feedback from the people who filled it out. The data becomes a tool for dialogue. The focus, rather than being stuck on the scores and comments, is on the much more important and positive task of how to move forward from here.

Furthermore, effective survey feedback is reciprocal. That is, the scores are understood to reflect a two-way street. If the boss scored low on workload prioritization, part of the puzzle is for subordinates that are confused about priorities to mention it to the boss, and to let the boss know what they understand or wish the priorities to be. This requires dialogue, with both parties taking ownership of their part in what is working and in what is not working so well. Such dialogue, on an ongoing basis, will take the organization to higher levels of performance with the side benefit of decreasing the reliance on outside experts.

Likewise, your people can give each other direct, timely individual feedback, and begin a continuous process of learning from their experiences and improving their skills. In high-performing groups and organizations, people talk directly to peers, bosses, subordinates, and other groups about what is working and what is not working. Any work team can move in this direction, and a critical mass in your organization of people who give and seek feedback grounded in specificity and ownership can quickly change the culture. You and your people are capable of direct and productive feedback.

2. Get the training, coaching, and facilitation necessary to make the transition to a culture of live group and individual feedback. Such work culture has been created time and again, and is directly related to high performance.

3. If you do the above, you will be creating positive, second-order change. With each moment of successful, live feedback, you and your people will be on a path of decreased blame and avoidance, increased trust, increased skill at handling difficult conversations, increased self-reliance (less need for facilitators, etc., as skills and confidence are embedded in the daily culture), and a step change in the willingness and ability to solve touchy problems that interfere with productivity.

Feedback is necessary. Anonymous feedback can actually have the unintended effect of decreasing the amount of live feedback flowing in the organization. Give yourself and your people the gift of skillful live feedback, and you will not only help them avoid the anonymous feedback blues, you will also get bottom line results.

The following is a framework for giving behaviorally specific feedback:

Behaviorally Specific Feedback

Giver:
A.   When you say or do _____, I feel _____.
Examples of feeling description:
Relieved, pleased, excited, proud, glad, thankful... I like it!
Or
Frustrated, concerned, afraid, surprised, upset, worried, defensive... I don't like it.
B.   What I want is _____.
C.   Is there something you want from me?

Receiver:
If emotion is running high (in you) while you receive, take a deep breath and make sure you understand the specifics of the feedback:
A.   Tell me more. What did I do or say? (Especially if they weren't specific!)
Or
B.   Paraphrase: Is this what you mean? When I said or did _____?
C.   Thank the person for having the courage to give you the feedback!

You don't have to agree with their version of what happened to appreciate the risk they are taking! If you want people to talk to you (instead of gossiping about you to others), you must manage your own reaction in such a way that they will be likely to approach you again in the future. Once burned...

Traps:
A.   Sharing negative judgments. As soon as you add "you were unprofessional" you are asking for a fight. Even positive judgments ("That was very professional") weaken the impact if they are not tied to behavior specifics ("When you did _____, it was...").
B.   Being sure you are "right!"
C.   Defending yourself without truly understanding their message! Make sure you understand even if the message is hard to hear! If you leap to explaining yourself when you feel defensive, you probably aren't really listening and that creates the likelihood that they won't listen either!
D.   If you think there is a misunderstanding that you want to clear up, ask if they are willing to listen, and then be behaviorally specific ("here's what I meant/think happened").

Figure 13.1 is a simple way to think about your subordinates' performance and organize your feedback for them.

This may not be in vogue, but to lead and supervise, you must *use your own judgment.* You are the only person your immediate reports are directly reporting to, and you need them to meet your expectations of

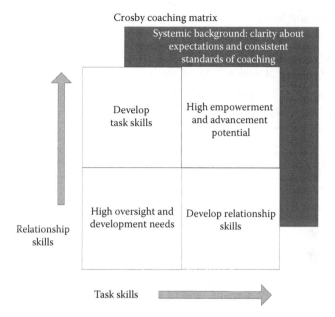

FIGURE 13.1
Crosby coaching matrix. (Created by the author using Visio.)

performance. If they are not, start with yourself and the system you are helping to create. Are you being clear? Are you doing a good job of connecting? Is there role and goal clarity? Are there factors, such as equipment conditions, impairing performance of the individuals and group(s) that you lead? As Kurt Lewin put it, "In summary one can say that behavior and development depend upon the state of the person and the environment B + F (P,E)." In other words, do what you can to create an environment that supports performance, including assessing your own impact on your subordinates, and with that in mind use your best judgment to assess the individuals who are working for you.

The matrix works like this. The left axis rates relationship skills. Are your subordinates interacting effectively with you, their peers, and the rest of the organization regarding work-related issues? Then they fall in the upper quadrants of the relationship-skills axis. The bottom axis rates task skills. Do they have the technical know-how to execute the required tasks? If they fall into the upper quadrant of both task and relationship, you are in good shape, can provide less oversight, and can focus on assisting them with their career aspirations. If they are lacking in either relationship or task skills or both, then that is where your development focus must be. If they are lacking in one or the other dimension and are unwilling or unable to respond in a timely manner to reasonable opportunities for development, then they may not be the right fit for your needs.

Take clear stands and stay connected, and most will respond, but not all. That is both the challenge and the burden of leadership. Hold yourself to the highest standards of supervisory effectiveness, and simultaneously give yourself permission to let go. Don't chase the stray cow.

14

Leading from Forming to High Performing

It should be noted that my father, Robert, contributed heavily to the section entitled "Stage 1," and my brother, Chris, to the ending section starting with "Stage 4."

Dr. Bruce Tuckman's model of group development has endured for decades as a simple way to understand group dynamics. His catchy and often quoted sequence is "form, storm, norm, and perform." He later added "adjourn." One reason for the popularity of his model is that it is easy to remember because it rhymes. Unfortunately, the word he chose for that very reason to describe conflict, "storm," is misunderstood by many to mean that an ugly fighting phase is necessary for a healthy group to develop. Another problem is that the model offers no guidelines on how to create a healthy (by which we mean high performing) group. The following approach, tested over decades of work with intact groups (i.e., boss and subordinates) and project teams, offers proven methods for actively guiding groups/teams, and indeed the entire organization, to high performance.

Like any good theory, Tuckman's model clarifies what we already know: it is predictable that in the beginning of any new group, there will be a period akin to a honeymoon stage, where members are focused on fitting in (*forming*), that eventually this need will be superseded by the surfacing of differences (the dramatic sounding *storming*), that how differences are managed will evolve into *norms* (Do we admit and explore differences? Do we fight about differences? Do we pretend as best we can that we don't have any differences?), and that these norms will impact group *performance*. In this light, Tuckman's stages are a useful predictor of group dynamics.

Unfortunately, the stages have been misunderstood by many as if they are to be simply endured. Most are unaware that research on Tuckman in 1975 by John Johnson noted, "Virtually all the studies that Tuckman reviewed, however, involved group leaders who were passive and nondirective and who made no attempt to intervene in group process." To be an effective leader you must take a much more active approach. While Tuckman's sequence raises awareness of the process that is unfolding, it's important to go beyond passive awareness. An effective leader must guide the group toward constructive ends rather than leaving group development to chance. Whether or not they are the formal leader, if even one group member knows the following methods, that group has a much stronger chance of achieving high performance.

Based on my experience with hundreds of groups over the past 30+ years, I propose that the active leadership stages of an effective group are

Stage 1: Inclusive forming/dispersed participation
Stage 2: Constructive storming/managing differences
Stage 3: Active norming/organizing the work
Stage 4: High-performing/self-renewing activities

It's important to note that even with a passive approach to Tuckman, the stages don't unfold in an entirely linear manner, nor in any set amount of time (for example, one is establishing norms from the very beginning, and conflict can, and will, emerge at any time). Rather, these are general guidelines and activities with an end goal of high performance.

To set the context of how this works, imagine yourself in a meeting. The meeting could be formal (a project team with members from every department) or informal (on the floor with two or three others). You may be a member or the person in charge. Regardless of your role or the circumstances of the meeting, Tuckman's stages are unfolding!

STAGE 1—INCLUSIVE FORMING

Even if you all know each other, you still must form as a group. There is no skipping stage 1, though of course if you've worked together often and well, stage 1 could be relatively easy. By taking an active rather than a passive approach, forming is a developmental stage that can be managed in order to ensure effective group dynamics and, ultimately, productive work.

Therefore, remake the first stage into "inclusive forming" because inclusion is the key component of the forming stage. Here's what to look for while forming, along with possible interventions toward the goal of constantly increasing the productivity of the group and any meeting. As mentioned, even if you seem to be the only one aware of these dynamic stages, you can likely help the others.

When you observe the group you notice that:

1. Some are being silent.
2. Someone comes late.
3. One person is constantly interrupted.
4. Another has a pattern of talking at great length.
5. And still another is new to the group.

These are forming, or, perhaps with the long talker, storming (control) issues in Tuckman's sequence. Inclusive forming holds a key to minimizing needless conflict and managing differences in a constructive manner during the storming phase.

In the order mentioned above, you might say (1) "Tom, is that issue of concern to you or those on your work crew?" (2) After the late one has settled in, "Mary just before you came in we were discussing…." (3) Some group members are more prone to wait and/or give their time to others. You must be active to bring them in. "Mike, I think you wanted to say something." (4) Those who talk long often repeat the same point over and over because they aren't sure if they are being understood. Risk interrupting after their first repetition and say, "Just a minute…I want to make sure I understand you and also that others get to comment. Do you mean that, '_____'? Did I get it?" "Yes? No? (Hopefully by now you recognize this as the active listening skill of paraphrasing covered in Appendix A.) Okay, but before you continue let's hear from others." (5) "Susan, welcome! In case anyone doesn't know, would you tell us your job responsibilities?"

The formal leader, or whoever is aware of these dynamics, can initiate bringing order and clarity in this beginning stage. There are also formal topics of inclusion, such as the team and meeting's purpose, current agenda, the team member's roles, etc. Of course, many are anxious when a meeting begins. Many are still thinking about unfinished tasks elsewhere. You can help them "arrive" and be present and engaged in the meeting.

Of course, the suggested statements above are merely illustrative. Each situation is unique. You will invent what is best for you, given your tendencies, your dominant conflict habits (confrontation, avoidance, etc.), and the urgency of the moment. The fundamental issues in stage 1 are as follows: How will this go for me and the group? If I am not the leader, how will the leader handle the group, including inclusion, conflict, and managing the task? Why am I here? Why are others? What is the purpose of this (formal or informal) gathering? Will anyone listen to me? Am I able to focus on what is happening here and now in the meeting including on what the other participants are saying, especially the new or quieter attendees when they risk speaking up? As goals and roles are clarified, who should be here and who is missing? Who speaks first? Is anyone listening in an active way? How do we help each bring their own unique expertise to bear on achieving our goals?

If you are aware of the importance of these group dynamics, you can then help bring clarity regarding the goals and roles of each participant, thus laying a foundation for high performance.

DISPERSED PARTICIPATION

Dispersed participation means tapping into the minds of all who are in the meeting and encouraging that they become engaged. It is about taking a clear stand by insisting on connection as a norm. It is living the value of wanting everyone's opinion and knowing that, if left to chance, this will be unlikely to occur, and the group's ability to pull off their business goals will be diminished.

Dispersed participation immediately begins establishing healthy norms around managing differences. Thus, you are actively navigating Tuckman's second and third stages from the very beginning. Establishing this norm involves adding structure, such as occasional pairings, to your meetings (see below) and will only happen if someone actively creates it. It is a blend of inclusive forming, constructive storming, and active norming. It is not so much a stage as it is a planned, evolving strategy to involve all as co-creators of the product of each meeting. It is a strategy that acknowledges that humans have a wide range of interactional patterns and need structure to have dispersed participation.

By some of the above-mentioned interventions, you (the reader) have already moved participation from a one- or two person-dominated meeting toward a meeting where the voices of all are more likely to be heard and reinforced as important.

In addition to the earlier, less formal suggestions, if you are the meeting leader, you will choose moments in the meeting to inject dispersed participation: "Here's our agenda. Take that first item and talk to the person beside you to warm up for our discussion." Or perhaps you will disperse participation by suggesting that they talk in pairs about whether there's any topic that needs to be added to the agenda. In a sense, you are inviting an organized "sidebar" conversation in order to engage everyone. The goal is to have everyone hear their own voice talking so as to reduce anxiety, especially with employees that are newer or lower in the hierarchy; to allow more introverted members a chance to think out loud but with some privacy (talking to one peer is a lot less threatening to most than is trying to articulate their view to an entire group); and to set a norm that engages all and invites all to take ownership of the outcomes.

Now who would resist this? Those who are stuck in a pattern of imbalanced participation. I've witnessed many leaders stuck in this pattern and blind to their role in it. They will do most of the talking in every interaction or meeting, and will often be silently frustrated that others aren't speaking more. It's an easy pattern to fall into, as most subordinates will defer to the highest authority figure's consumption of air time. Subordinates will be reluctant to interrupt, and will be practiced at looking as if they are listening, even when their attention has started to wander. As a leader, don't accept the invitation to perpetuate this pattern. Pay attention to the balance of who is speaking, and find ways to encourage dispersed participation. Who else will resist? Those subordinates that have taken on the systemic role of speaking up in a meeting where participation is not dispersed.

Example: Imagine a meeting with 50 employees attending. The manager who has called the meeting talks for a while and then asks, "Any questions?" Who speaks when the manager asks this, or, if the custom is to do so, who raises their hands? In our experience, there are usually two or three in the audience who will speak up first and do most, or even all, of the talking. They speak and the leader feels obligated to respond. If you recognize this as the stray cow syndrome from Chapter 5, you are correct.

What's worse for the leader that is unintentionally co-creating this, since wider participation is not the norm, these few are likely to represent any hostility resident in the group. They are likely to do so in an angry, blaming way, and be seen as heroes by some of their peers. These few will "resist" participation being dispersed.

Of course, it's easier to change this dynamic if you are the leader rather than just a member. As a member, you would be wise to wait and make this and related suggestions privately to the leader before the next meeting, rather than try to control such dynamics on your own. Put yourself in the leader's shoes: it's easier to receive "corrective" feedback (even if it is simply intended as helpful) privately than publicly. And it will be less awkward for you if the leader rejects your suggestion. To the leader, here is what I suggest.

Begin with a brief statement about the agenda or a key issue. Then say, "Discuss this with someone beside you and in a few minutes I would like to hear what you think." Do not ask if this is ok! Immediately turn your back, avert your eyes, or do whatever you need to do to not get sucked into immediately engaging with the two or three who do not want their influence to be diffused (walk out of the room, take a sip of water, turn and talk to a colleague, etc.).

In many cases, just asking the participants to turn and say or do something like that suggested above will be enough for them to do it, but in extreme cases like illustrated above, you will need to be firm. I've seen these few raise their hands vigorously and even shout their objections in an attempt to try and stop such pairings. Consciously or not, they may anxiously want to maintain their status as the spokespersons. They speak in "we" language as if they represent all! Rarely do they speak for themselves. Also, many silent employees are glad to empower the few who speak so they can stay safely on the sidelines. The purpose here is not to end dissent, but rather to empower all to join in the co-creation of the group or meeting and to do so in a problem-solving, not a blaming, way.

Three or four minutes are long enough (although if people are obviously engaged in their paired conversations, you might wisely give them more time). Now you have a next critical intervention. "Okay, I want to hear what you're thinking. Speak for yourself. Someone over there start (pointing in a direction away from the vocal few)." Ask for comments, not questions. If you ask, "Does anyone have any questions?" the likelihood is that even those who have clear opinions will voice it in the form of a question ("Do you really think that is a good idea?") and you will waste time trying to answer when you could have been in dialogue about what they actually think. Knowing where people stand is much more likely to be productive.

By creating dispersed participation through the methods above, I have often witnessed large meetings go from a few participating to a much broader participation in a short period of time. Leaders are often amazed and thankful. It may not be easy at first, but the tyranny of the cocreated stray cow syndrome must be broken if you are to move to the next stage in a productive way.

STAGE 2—CONSTRUCTIVE STORMING/ MANAGING DIFFERENCES

As mentioned, storming, while a handy word because it rhymes, tends to evoke unfortunate images of dramatic conflict. My brother (and colleague) witnessed faculty in a graduate program actually get upset with a highly functioning group because they didn't appear to be "storming," and mark them down based on the criticism "how could they be a healthy group?" That is a common misunderstanding of Tuckman. While intense confrontation may happen in any relationship, differences can also be managed effectively without dramatics. Stage 2 in Tuckman's model is primarily about the shift in the group's dynamics from a predictable and understandable focus on fitting in (managing initial anxiety by focusing on similarities and on the leader) to noticing and addressing differences. It is the end of the honeymoon phase. This happens when people begin to feel comfortable. Ironically, it is this very sense of becoming comfortable with the group that increases anxiety, as one begins to note differences. "I'm just starting to feel good about this...why rock the boat by bringing that up?" An active leader, using the methods already outlined, can help the group past any such anxiety by maintaining norms of inclusion and dispersed participation, and by openly valuing the surfacing and exploration of differences.

A fundamental key to this stage lies in one's beliefs about conflict. Many, especially in the early stages of beginning to be a member of a group (and again in the adjourning stage), fear conflict will fracture the group, or at least their relationship to it. It is tempting to play it safe and avoid "rocking the boat." In contrast, the theory here is that differences between any two people, and certainly in a group, are inevitable, and if managed well are a source of higher performance.

Toyota's culture is a prime example. Their climb to high quality and performance was built upon immediately praising employees for bringing production problems to management's attention (a vital cultural detail ironically overlooked by many adapting the Toyota system and/or Lean manufacturing). Upon review, you and the group are not going to put time and effort into every problem raised, but it is far better to be aware of potential issues than to be ignorant of them. If the attempt to raise concerns is met with defensiveness and other forms of push-back, then all but the most persistent group members will stop trying. Information and engagement will be lost. The likelihood of high performance will diminish.

This is the critical juncture for the group and nowhere is the shadow of the leader cast more strongly than in the management of conflict. As objectively as possible, a wise leader is clear about their own beliefs about conflict, and manages conflict in a manner that is best for group performance, even if it in some ways runs counter to their own beliefs. Conflict, according to noted expert Dr. Jay Hall, "is a natural part of human interaction…the way we, as individuals, think about and choose to handle conflict is more important in determining its outcome than the nature of the conflict itself" (Hall, 1969). Dr. Hall goes on to say that conflict itself is neither good nor bad: what matters is how we think about it and manage it. A simple way to think about it is that a conflict is any differences, whether large or small, whether high or low in emotional intensity, that matter to either party. Ignoring small "differences," while tempting, often leads to even more complicated clashes down the road, or to avoidance of issues and/or individuals. Surfacing differences about work issues is far better for performance than driving them underground.

Of equal or greater importance as one's beliefs, and related to them, is one's behavior. We all have habits when managing conflict. An accurate understanding of your behavioral tendencies allows you to not be limited by them. For example, is it easy to give you feedback, or do your reactions make it difficult? Ideally, you are able to calmly listen and make sure you really understand even when the person raising an issue is doing so in a less than polished or stellar manner. A master of conflict can help the parties involved (including themselves) get to clarity, even if they initially feel defensive and upset by the topic or the manner in which it was raised.

In sum, to navigate stage 2, a wise leader assesses his or her own beliefs and behaviors, and does the work necessary to overcome his or her own shortcomings, such as seeking feedback and skill building. With a patient and nondefensive approach, with norms of inclusion and dispersed participation, Tuckman's phase 2 can unfold smoothly, without high drama. And if there are some fireworks, or difficult conflicts, the team will be much better positioned to move forward, trusting that they can handle any difficulties that emerge.

STAGE 3—ACTIVE NORMING

As an active leader, if you have followed our guidance, you have already established "norms" by now of inclusion, dispersed participation, and of calmly and intentionally surfacing differences. There will always be some norms in any group that the members are unaware of, but taking an active role makes it far more likely that the norms in your group will support high performance. In contrast, a passive approach might lead to performance barriers, such as members being alienated and underutilized, or important topics being avoided. Besides the norms we have already covered, there are others that consistently support high group and organization performance. Table 14.1 (from Robert P. Crosby's "Solving the Crosswork Puzzle") illustrates such norms.

These characteristics apply to groups as well as to whole systems. For the purpose of your group, it's very important that you have clear and

TABLE 14.1

Characteristics of Healthy and Unhealthy Systems

Dimension	Unhealthy System	Healthy System
Management	Frantic	Centered
Influence	None	Appropriate
Alignment	Not well aligned	Well aligned
Communication	Gossip—closed	Openness and dialogue
Consequence management	Capricious discipline	Clear consequence
Decision making	Consistently extreme (either consensual or authoritarian)	Flexible and clear
Interactive skill	Low	High
Task goals	Unclear	Clear
Accountability	Fuzzy	Single-point
Implementation	Poor	Effective
Rewards	None	Appropriate
Sponsorship	Poor	Clear

aligned sponsorship from every boss that has a member in the group. This sponsorship should be traced to a single point in the organization (the initiating sponsor) to the extent possible (trickier, if not all members are from the same organization, for example). The measurable outcomes to be achieved by the group must also be clear and understood by all members and bosses sponsoring a group member. This work on clarity and alignment is often minimized or even skipped, and if so, it always results in a significant barrier to the group achieving its goals.

Hand in hand with sponsorship alignment, and again often neglected, is role clarity (including time commitment/management) and consequence management if group members and/or their superiors fail to support needed and agreed upon activity (see Chapter 13). The initiating sponsor must monitor these dynamics and overall progress, or effectively delegate that monitoring, if they want the group to succeed (for more on our definition of "sponsorship," see Chapter 10).

The ability to monitor and the likelihood of progress depend on yet another of the characteristics graphed above: a commitment to single point accountability for decisions and tasks (who will do and decide what by when). Further decision clarity, such as who needs to be consulted prior to key decisions and who needs to be informed, is also vital (for more on decision-making clarity, see Chapter 12 and Stage 4 below). This clarity must be driven both by the team leader and the initiating sponsor.

Along with inclusion, dispersed participation, and constructive management of conflict, the above are minimum norms necessary if you want your group to succeed. If not, why bother forming the group in the first place?

STAGE 4—HIGH-PERFORMANCE/ SELF-RENEWING ACTIVITIES

High performance is not a given, but if you have followed the path outlined thus far, it is likely. By successfully influencing your group dynamics your team will be characterized by balanced participation, calm and consistent surfacing of differences and issues relevant to group and task performance, adequate support from the organization, as well as a high degree of clarity about goals, roles, tasks and decisions. Ultimately the work will be done on time and with quality. The challenge becomes how to maintain high performance.

With successful work in the first three stages of group development, you have established norms for high productivity. Now you must continuously tweak the group dynamics. For instance, if many have been contributing, you may have discovered more real issues. You can deliberately "capture" these and record them for problem-solving, perhaps by a small subgroup with particular interest and knowledge about an issue. Also, you are hearing from each other and learning more about the various roles of each. Role clarity is critical for the effectiveness of the individual, but it is equally important that each member know what to expect from the other. Otherwise, time is wasted asking others to do what is not expected of them.

However, if you've broadened participation, there are likely to be other stumbling blocks. Some will believe that they now will be in on every decision. The two extremes of authoritarianism and anarchy are familiar. The middle styles (consultative and delegative...introduced in Chapter 12) are rarely understood or even known. The belief developed, perhaps, in one's growing-up years, is that either the boss (parent) decides or it's up for grabs. Aware of this common developmental belief, a productive work group spends enough time to clarify who decides, who influences, and how that influence impacts many, but not all, decisions. The leader of the group should keep an eye on delegating decision authority to the employees as they become more competent and are in need of quick decisions, but always in a way that adds structure and clarity, versus chaos and anarchy.

Without broadening participation through the dispersed participation methods mentioned above, much of the information held by the employees will not be shared. Once the norm of everyone speaking up is clearly established, then you can be more intentional about who speaks on what topic. Those with direct knowledge on the topic that is being discussed need to be engaged and express their specific data and opinions. Dispersed participation does not require that everyone speaks on every topic. That would be tiresome and highly inefficient. With clarity about the roles and skills of each group member, who is more knowledgeable about differing issues will become apparent. This will not be based on hierarchy, but on expertise.

A final critical component of high performance is problem-solving in a disciplined, participative way, which, of course, includes follow-through. As with who speaks about which topics, participative problem-solving does not mean using all people to problem-solve all issues. Instead, it means involving those with the most knowledge, both technical and hands-on, in solving the problems. These may be on your team or outside your team. A common mistake is to overlook the knowledge of hourly workers while trying to solve problems that they deal with every day. Not only are they a rich source of information, but also their participation in problem-solving makes successful implementation of solutions much more likely, for both technical and emotional reasons. To ignore these dynamics is folly, and yet they get ignored in most organizations every day. Disciplined problem-solving requires using an effective methodology that helps ensure that all relevant data is surfaced and worked on in an effective way. Once the norms for high performance are in place, the actual method of problem-solving becomes less important.

Although there are many such methods, I favor "force-field analysis" by Kurt Lewin because it addresses the systemic dynamic of homeostasis (or in Lewin's words, "equilibrium") and can be facilitated in a highly participative manner (as was done in the earlier illustration of the bauxite refinery's cross-functional planning session). As Lewin put it, "it is of great practical importance that levels of quasi-stationary equilibria can be changed in either of two ways: by adding forces in the desired direction or by diminishing opposing forces...In both cases, the equilibrium might change to the same new level. The secondary effect should, however, be quite different. In the first case the process on the new level would be accompanied by a state of relatively high tension, in the second case, by a state of relatively low tension. Since increase of tension above a certain degree is likely to be paralleled by higher aggressiveness, higher emotionality, and lower constructiveness, it is clear that as a rule, the second method would be preferable." In other words, in force-field analysis, rather than just coming up with solutions ("adding forces in the desired direction"), the group also identifies barriers to success ("opposing forces") and creates strategies to address them. I have seen this method play a role in successful implementations time and again.

Finally, follow-through is essential to success and requires more discipline than most leaders and organizations seem to realize. In *Cultural Change in Organizations*, Appendix A—"Do You Really Want Change: Eleven Do's and Don'ts for Those Who Are Serious," my brother, Chris Crosby, put it this way:

Be Serious About Follow-Up

Many treat events and task lists as the end product of change rather than an important step toward achieving a desired result. If you check off a list of tasks and expect that to get you to your end game, then you are missing the point. Tasks are merely a hypothesis about what will solve a problem. Follow-up is the process of driving tasks to completion and making sure you obtain your stated objective. Don't stop the process if you have little or no results. Create a new hypothesis and test it until the problem is really solved. This takes time, diligence, patience, and commitment. Ironically, without it, you will waste more time by living with problems and poor processes, which could be solved by effective follow-up.

Bottom line: You are not serious about change until you are serious about follow-up.

Self-Renewing Activities

Self-renewing activities are about looking at how your group is functioning as a unit, and making small adjustments to maintain or improve your level of performance. It amounts to holding up a mirror to your group's overall performance and choosing what needs to be different, so that productive work continues to happen. It is a stage intended to extend the "performing" sequence of Tuckman's model indefinitely.

Professional sports teams understand this stage and spend more time practicing their plays and reflecting on them than actually playing. Yet work groups rarely, if ever, practice or reflect about how they are working together in a disciplined way. This stage does not have to be difficult; the trick is to make sure it happens. There are many ways to do this. One of the most effective is for the group to self-assess by using a survey and then having an immediate dialogue about improving performance (my father's first organization development book, *Walking the Empowerment Tightrope*, is dedicated to this topic and provides step-by-step guidance). This may sound like a contradiction of my stand in the last chapter on 360 surveys, but it actually is not. Anonymous ratings can fuel open and direct feedback if they are used as a springboard for dialogue. For example, a group might anonymously rate on a one to ten scale whether they are getting what they need from other groups (or each other, or their boss, etc.). They may need a skilled facilitator (periodically that is wise for even the highest performing groups … just like a coach is wise for a sports team) to help them have the most productive conversation possible. This may surprise you, but whether the group rated an item high or low is in a sense irrelevant. What's important is the dialogue about the particular item/topic in terms of whether it needs improvement and if so who is going to do what and by when. A few hours of effective self-assessment and dialogue can empower a group toward higher performance for six months or a year.

With or without a survey, the questions to focus on are simple: What's working? What's not? Are the goals clear? Do the measurements quantify what the work team thinks is relevant? Are the roles clear, wisely defined, and known to each other? Are the group members getting what they want from the leader? Are resources readily available?

By asking questions such as these, or others that you determine are important, and problem-solving with the total work group, you will take your group dynamics and performance to another level.

Creating a high-performance group is hard work, but achievable. For a small minority, it comes easily (and many who think they are masters of group leadership have significant blind spots), but for most it takes intentional learning and strategy. Many have been able to achieve predictable results when working with groups utilizing these concepts. The cost of not doing this work gets reflected directly in the bottom line. Work groups and meetings held within these parameters tend to create motivated employees who feel valued, understand the issues, contribute to problem solving, have clarity about roles and goals, and work harder to achieve results.

By actively navigating Tuckman's stages as inclusive forming, constructive storming, active norming, and high performing/self-renewing, leaders and group members have choices and interventions they can take to be more effective. Leaders who have clear expectations of group and organization behavior; who learn these skills and strategies in-depth; and who demonstrate, encourage, and insist on healthy norms in their groups and throughout the organization, increase their leadership effectiveness and consistently get results.

15

Self-Differentiated Leadership

Congratulations. You've come a long ways since the beginning of this book. Hopefully you are not feeling overwhelmed. Leadership may seem complicated when you try to take into account group dynamics, goal alignment, decision clarity, emotional intelligence, etc. The good news is the essential leadership theory at the core of this book is powerful precisely because it is simple enough to be drawn on in almost any situation: take clear stands and stay connected.

The other message that I hope you are getting loud and clear is *be yourself*. Only you can determine what you really stand for/care about, and only you can be genuinely you, which is critical to connecting. Do the self-analysis that is woven throughout this book. Find your adult essence. As one of my father's mentors, Howard Thurman, put it: "There is something in every one of you that waits and listens for the sound of the genuine inside yourself. It is the only true guide you will ever have. And if you cannot hear it, you will all of your life spend your days on the ends of strings that somebody else pulls" (Thurman, 2006).

Being genuine doesn't mean always saying what you think. We all have thoughts that are best not said. Take the high road. Don't settle for less, such as "genuinely" being a person who doesn't listen, for example. Strive to be the way you really want to be, and be honest with yourself and with others as you do so.

Be transparent about what you are working on in terms of your own self-development. Humility in a leader goes a long way in terms of connecting, and also sets a powerful standard in terms of others working on themselves. Paradoxically, take clear stands (even if you do this privately, in your head) about boundaries that are important to you. Transparency doesn't mean you reveal everything you think and feel, or that you are available to everyone all of the time. You must decide what degree of privacy meets your needs and protects your energy. As the following ten statements indicate, self-differentiation is a uniquely personal task. They complete the sentence that starts "self-differentiation is:"

- Being clear about one's own personal values and goals
- Taking maximum responsibility for one's own emotional being and destiny rather than blaming others or the context
- Charting one's own way by means of one's own internal guidance system, rather than perpetually eyeing the "scope" to see where others are at
- Knowing where one ends and another begins
- The capacity to take a stand in an intense emotional system
- Saying "I" when others are demanding "we"
- Being able to cease being one of the system's emotional dominoes
- Maintaining a non-anxious presence in the face of others
- Containing one's reactivity to the reactivity of others
- A lifetime project, with no one ever getting more than 70% of the way to the goal (from "Bowen Theory and Therapy" by Edwin Friedman in the *Handbook of Family Therapy, Volume II*, edited by Gurman and Kniskern, 1991)

I want to elaborate on two of these (I'm hoping by now the rest are fairly straightforward). By "maintaining a non-anxious presence in the face of anxious others," Friedman doesn't mean you will never feel anxious. Anxiety in the right dose is an important self-motivating emotion. What he does mean is that you will be a calming presence when the going gets tough and emotional intensity is running high in others. You will be the step-down transformer in the emotional system, so that your people can focus on and execute the task at hand.

By "a lifetime project, with no one ever getting more than 70 percent of the way to the goal," Friedman doesn't mean you will never get there. From what I have read, I believe he meant that even the best of us, Mahatma Gandhi or any leader you think was dynamic at taking clear stands and connecting, will only be self-differentiated 70% of the time. The rest of the time even the best will stumble into reactive behavior. You will be 100% differentiated at times, and fused (and confused) at others. Give yourself a break when it happens, learn what you can from the experience, and as a colleague of mine, Denny Minno, used to say, "It's not what you do, it's what you do next that matters." As long as you are still ticking and have some humility, you can make amends and improve yourself. How else could leadership be learned?

As Friedman puts it in *Generation to Generation*, "The basic concept of leadership through self-differentiation is this: If a leader will take primary responsibility for his or her own position as 'head' and work to define his or her own goals and self, while *staying in touch* with the rest of the organism, there is a more than reasonable chance that the body will follow. There may be initial resistance but, if the leader can stay in touch with the resisters, the body will usually go along."

Be "the head" not for ego but because the body can't function without it. Human beings are born into authority relationships, and effective authority is vital to organizing human activity. Authority is not the problem. Reactivity to authority is the problem. Be the best leader, follower, and peer you can be and you will create high performance. Relate to everyone with respect as a human being, and support everyone in their roles, including yourself.

Be clear, but don't cut off. Engage the resisters, put them to work removing barriers if you can, but don't trap yourself by waiting for everyone to be happy about the direction you are headed. Prepare yourself and your people as best you can, set goals based on the best information available, gather your courage, and enter the forest. To do so is not an act of certainty. To do so is a leap of faith.

Again, the words of Howard Thurman: "Faith is an action...a leap not to belief in a doctrine...but to a way of being...a leap across a chasm of unknowing! And always within me there is the rumor that I may be wrong! And that's my growing edge!" (Thurman, 2006).

Respecting that rumor is a wise act of humility. If you have no doubts, you wouldn't be human. But don't let your doubts hold you back. The reality is only time will tell what will happen next, and that is why true acts of leadership will always take an adventurous spirit. By taking clear stands and staying connected, you will be well equipped to pull it off.

Finally, if you haven't yet, read Appendix A. The skill building activities there are priceless aids for interpersonal and leadership effectiveness. Appendix B is a quiz that can also be used as a checklist of leadership behaviors essential to effectiveness. Keep learning and keep leading! It's been a privilege to assist you on your journey!

Appendix A:
Four Key Skills*

Wallen identified four skills that are helpful in closing or minimizing interpersonal gaps: They are

- Behavior description
- Feeling description
- Perception check
- Paraphrase

BEHAVIOR DESCRIPTION

The first skill, behavior description, is essential to self-awareness and to being open with others while being as inoffensive as possible. As mentioned, it is also essential to effective supervision. The challenge is to be aware of the words and actions to which we are reacting. This is more difficult than it sounds. Most people generalize ("You don't trust me") when what they mean, of course, is "based on what you did and/or said, I have come to the belief that you don't trust me." If you can be precise about what it was that was done or said ("You told me not to step on the ice"), you can get clearer about what you are reacting to, and choose whether to offer the information to the other. If you tell people your interpretations of them, they will likely be offended and go into fight or flight mode. If you can tell them what it was that they did or said that led to your reaction, you are both more likely to learn from the interaction, and come to a mutual understanding.

Too often interpersonal effectiveness suffers as a result of language that, although intended as factual, is subject to various interpretations. Engineers in their reports, supervisors in giving feedback, parents in their discipline, quality inspectors, employees attempting to be clear about concerns, all confuse phrases that make a judgment from those that report

---

* Excerpted with permission from "*Fight, Flight, Freeze: Emotional Intelligence, Behavioral Science, Systems Theory & Leadership,*" Gil Crosby, Second Edition, CrosbyOD Publishing, Seattle, WA, 2015.

a fact (as close to an objective description of a behavior or condition as possible), and this confusion often gives rise to conflict: "You're being careless" versus "Three jars were broken this past hour." "The second shift isn't working as hard" versus "Production is down 40 cases today compared to yesterday." A skillful person strives to communicate with specificity. They get it that a judgment/interpretation not only inflames, but worse it draws attention and energy away from the problem (i.e., three jars were broken) and toward the feelings of the accused and to the accusation itself.

Activity: John Wallen designed the quiz in figure below. Take it to hone your understanding of behavior description. The goal of the quiz is to distinguish between behaviorally specific statements and interpretations. Review the eighteen statements in the quiz and put an X beside the one that you consider to be observable data (words or actions) versus interpretations (the observer's beliefs about the words and actions).

Behavior Description Quiz

1. ___ Joe was not being professional.
2. ___ Harry was not sincere.
3. ___ Harry misinterpreted Joe.
4. ___ Joe was discouraged.
5. ___ Harry's voice got louder when he said, "Cut it out, Joe."
6. ___ Joe was trying to make Harry mad.
7. ___ Harry talked more than Joe did.
8. ___ Joe was aggressive.
9. ___ Joe said nothing when Harry said, "Cut it out."
10. ___ Harry knew that Joe was feeling discouraged.
11. ___ Joe talked about the weather and the baseball game.
12. ___ Jane deliberately changed the subject.
13. ___ Bill forgot the meeting.
14. ___ Harry didn't show respect to his boss.
15. ___ That's the third time you've started to talk while I was talking.
16. ___ The furnace repair was inadequate.
17. ___ Harry did not look me in the eyes when he spoke to me.
18. ___ Joe said, "I expect to receive this report by 3:00 PM tomorrow."

Behavior description quiz. (All materials in Appendix A are excerpted with permission from *Fight, Flight, Freeze: Emotional Intelligence, Behavioral Science, Systems Theory & Leadership*, Gil Crosby, Third Edition, CrosbyOD Publishing, Seattle, WA, 2015, including materials created by Dr. John Wallen, which are accessed through the public domain.)

ANSWERS TO BEHAVIOR DESCRIPTION QUIZ

1. Joe was not being professional—*interpretation.*

   The word "professional" is a value judgment (generally the above statement is delivered as a criticism, with the deliverer valuing "professionalism"). It is an interpretation of behavior, not an observable action or statement. Observable actions and/ or statements are as close as we can get to "facts." While there may be general cultural agreement on what it means to be a "professional" (i.e., courteous, punctual, reliable, etc.), there are wide differences about how those general expectations translate into moment-to-moment daily behavior. Do you interrupt a meeting because of an urgent matter? Is that professional (getting things done) or rude? As with all interpretations, the judgment is in the eye of the beholder (this is true whether only one person judges a behavior in a particular way, or whether everyone on the planet judges it the same way). Going back to Joe, if someone wants to influence Joe (to be "more professional"), they must be behaviorally specific ("interrupt, if you think it's necessary," or "never interrupt, whatever it is will have to wait"). Joe probably thinks he is professional, so without behavioral specificity, all they will accomplish is to insult him.

2. Harry was not sincere—*interpretation.*

   We can never know for sure if a person is sincere or insincere. We can observe that they aren't looking us in the eye; we can see that they aren't smiling; we can hear that they repeated themselves, etc. Interactions are rich with observable data. We may guess that someone is sincere or insincere based on the data. That is an interpretation; based on data—it is not a scientific fact.

3. Harry misinterpreted Joe—*interpretation.*

   It could be an accurate interpretation. Any interpretation could be accurate. But again we are making up a story based on what we have observed. The story could be inaccurate.

   The common mistake that people make is to believe that their interpretations, and the interpretations of trusted others, are facts, and to lose sight that there are other possibilities.

4. Joe was discouraged—*interpretation.*

   This is a guess about Joe's emotional state, undoubtedly inferred from statements and other behaviors (facial expression, tone of voice, posture. etc.), but a guess nonetheless.

5. Harry's voice got louder when he said, "Cut it out, Joe"—*behavior description.*

   This is all based on observable data. You can hear a person's voice get louder, and you can hear their words. No interpretations (such as "Harry was unprofessional," or "Harry wasn't sure that Joe heard him") were added.

6. Joe was trying to make Harry mad—*interpretation.*

   Here we are guessing at Joe's intentions. This type of judgment is more often than not way off base, and even if unspoken adds tension to the relationship between the judger (in this case, whoever is forming this interpretation of Joe) and the person being judged.

7. Harry talked more than Joe did—*behavior description.*

   That's simply a fact: Somebody talked more than the other. There's no value judgment added in this sentence. An observer may judge either or both of them based on the behavior that has been described ("Joe is timid," "Joe is polite," "Harry is domineering," etc.), but such interpretations are not included in the above sentence. Rather, they are in the eye of the beholder.

8. Joe was aggressive—*interpretation.*

   What appears to be "aggressive" behavior is admired as "assertive" by another. Sometimes a behavior by a woman is called "aggressive" (or worse), whereas that same behavior by a man is called "assertive" or "manly." So the same behavior can be admired or not depending on how it fits our prejudice (prejudgment) of how a certain person or type of person "should" behave.

9. Joe said nothing when Harry said, "Cut it out"—*behavior description.*
   Harry's words and Joe's silence are observable behavior.

10. Harry knew that Joe was feeling discouraged—*interpretation.*

11. Joe talked about the weather and the baseball game—*behavior description.*

12. Jane deliberately changed the subject—*interpretation.*

   Jane may have changed the subject, but without further information (such as asking Jane) whether she did so deliberately is a matter of interpretation.

13. Bill forgot the meeting—*interpretation.*

    Bill didn't attend the meeting may be a fact. Whether he forgot, only Bill knows for sure.

14. Harry didn't show respect to his boss—*interpretation.*

    Respect means different things to different people. For example, for some, it's a sign of respect if people will tell them when they are angry with them, while others believe anger is disrespectful.

15. That's the third time you've started to talk while I was talking—*behavior description.*

16. The furnace repair was inadequate—*interpretation.*

17. Harry did not look me in the eyes when he spoke to me—*behavior description.*

18. Joe said, "I expect to receive this report by 3:00 PM tomorrow"—*behavior description.*

Good work!

FEELING DESCRIPTION

Now that you're sharpening your ability to be behaviorally specific, it's time to work on being clearer and more specific about your own emotions. To assist in this process, the figure shows a list, by no means exhaustive, of words used to describe emotion (divided into the four emotional "food groups" of sad, mad, glad, and afraid—you can think of all emotions as being more or less intense versions of these four).

SAD

High intensity ⬅————————➡ Low intensity

Depressed	Grim	Dejected	Shame	Cheerless
Devastated	Melancholy	Discouraged	Solemn	Disappointed
Disconsolate	Mournful	Dismal	Sullen	Embarrassed
Empty	Sorrowful	Dispirited	Unhappy	Hurt
Grieving	Woebegone	Down		Pained
Hopeless	Woeful	Downcast		Somber
Helpless	Blue	Heavy		
	Bleak	Lonely		
	Crestfallen	Morose		

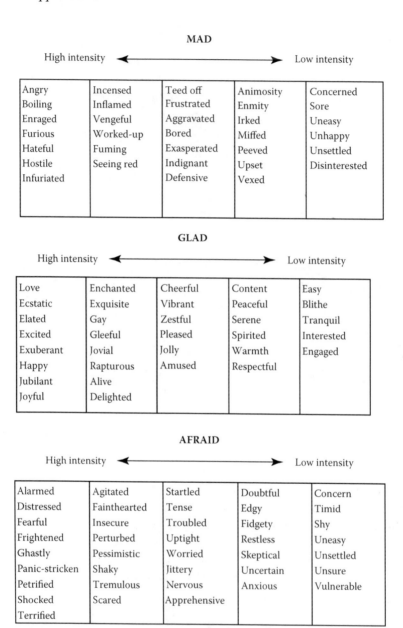

MAD

High intensity ←————————————→ Low intensity

Angry	Incensed	Teed off	Animosity	Concerned
Boiling	Inflamed	Frustrated	Enmity	Sore
Enraged	Vengeful	Aggravated	Irked	Uneasy
Furious	Worked-up	Bored	Miffed	Unhappy
Hateful	Fuming	Exasperated	Peeved	Unsettled
Hostile	Seeing red	Indignant	Upset	Disinterested
Infuriated		Defensive	Vexed	

GLAD

High intensity ←————————————→ Low intensity

Love	Enchanted	Cheerful	Content	Easy
Ecstatic	Exquisite	Vibrant	Peaceful	Blithe
Elated	Gay	Zestful	Serene	Tranquil
Excited	Gleeful	Pleased	Spirited	Interested
Exuberant	Jovial	Jolly	Warmth	Engaged
Happy	Rapturous	Amused	Respectful	
Jubilant	Alive			
Joyful	Delighted			

AFRAID

High intensity ←————————————→ Low intensity

Alarmed	Agitated	Startled	Doubtful	Concern
Distressed	Fainthearted	Tense	Edgy	Timid
Fearful	Insecure	Troubled	Fidgety	Shy
Frightened	Perturbed	Uptight	Restless	Uneasy
Ghastly	Pessimistic	Worried	Skeptical	Unsettled
Panic-stricken	Shaky	Jittery	Uncertain	Unsure
Petrified	Tremulous	Nervous	Anxious	Vulnerable
Shocked	Scared	Apprehensive		
Terrified				

Feeling words. (All materials in Appendix A is excerpted with permission from *Fight, Flight, Freeze: Emotional Intelligence, Behavioral Science, Systems Theory & Leadership,* Gil Crosby, Third Edition, CrosbyOD Publishing, Seattle, WA, 2015.)

Of course, which words match what feeling and what level of intensity is in the eye of the beholder (another interpretation!). Circle the words you use when naming your emotions, or (if they are absent) add the words you use to the list.

One way that we filter the truth that we are conveying to others (and possibly fool ourselves, as well) is to use low-intensity words to describe high-intensity emotions. Are you aware of doing this? Make a mental note of it.

Next, complete Exercise F-1, by John Wallen.

EXERCISE F-1

INTRODUCTION

Any spoken statement can convey feelings. Even the factual report, "It's three o'clock" can be said so that it expresses anger or disappointment. However, it is not the words that convey the feelings. Whether the statement is perceived as a factual report or as a message of anger or disappointment is determined by the speaker's tone, emphasis, gestures, posture, and facial expression. This exercise does not deal with the nonverbal ways that we express feelings. Rather, it focuses on the kinds of verbal statements we use to communicate feelings.

We convey feeling by

- Commands: "Get out!" or "Shut up!"
- Questions: "Is it safe to drive this fast?"
- Accusations: "You only think about yourself!"
- Judgments: "You're a wonderful person" or "You're too bossy."

Notice that, although each of the examples conveys strong feeling, the statement does not say what the feeling is. In fact, none of the sentences even refers to the speaker or what he or she is feeling.

By contrast, the emotional state of the speaker is the content of some sentences. Such sentences will be called "description of feeling." They convey feeling by naming or identifying what the speaker feels:

- "I am disappointed."
- "I am furiously angry!"
- "I'm afraid going this fast!"
- "I feel discouraged."

The goal of this exercise is to help you recognize when you are describing your feelings and when you are conveying feelings without describing them. Trying to describe what you are feeling is a helpful way to become more aware of what it is you do feel. A description of feeling conveys maximum information about what you feel in a way that will probably be less hurtful than commands, questions, accusations, and judgments. Thus, when you want to communicate your feelings more accurately, you will be able to do so.

PROCEDURE

Complete only one item at a time, as the steps show.

1. Mark your answers for item 1 only; do NOT do items 2, 3, etc., yet.
2. Compare your responses to item 1 with your learning partner(s) (if working alone, skip this step). Discuss the reasons for any differences.
3. Turn to "Discussion of Responses to Exercise F-1." Read and discuss item 1 only.
4. Repeat steps for item 2. Then continue this process for each item in turn until you have completed all ten items.

The sets of sentences in Exercise F-1 (see figure on next page) convey feelings. Each sentence in a set, however, may be communicating the same feelings using different methods. Put a "D" before each sentence that conveys the feeling by describing the speaker's feeling. Put a "NO" before each sentence that *conveys* the feeling, but does not describe the speaker's feeling.

1. (___) a. Shut up! not another word out of you!
    (___) b. I'm really annoyed by what you just said.

2. (___) a. Can't you see I'm busy? Don't you have eyes?
    (___) b. I'm beginning to resent your frequent interruptions.
    (___) c. You have no consideration for anyone else's feelings. You're completely selfish.

3. (___) a. I feel discouraged because of some of the things that happened today.
    (___) b. This has been an awful day.

4. (___) a. You're a wonderful person.
    (___) b. I really respect your opinion. You're so well-read.

5. (___) a. I feel comfortable and free to be myself when I'm around you.
    (___) b. We all feel you're a wonderful person.
    (___) c. Everybody likes you.

6. (___) a. If things don't improve around here, I'll look for a new job.
    (___) b. Did you ever hear of such a lousy place to work?
    (___) c. I'm afraid to admit that I need help with my work.

7. (___) a. This is a very poor exercise.
    (___) b. I feel this is a very poor exercise.

8. (___) a. I feel inadequate to contribute anything to this group.
    (___) b. I am inadequate to contribute anything to this group.

9. (___) a. I am a failure; I'll never amount to anything.
    (___) b. That teacher is awful; he didn't teach me anything.
    (___) c. I'm depressed because I did so poorly on that test.

10. (___) a. I feel lonely and isolated in my group.
    (___) b. For all of the attention anybody pays to what I say I might as well not be in my group.
    (___) c. I feel that nobody in my group cares whether I am there or not.

Feeling description quiz. (All materials in Appendix A are excerpted with permission from *Fight, Flight, Freeze: Emotional Intelligence, Behavioral Science, Systems Theory & Leadership*, Gil Crosby, Third Edition, CrosbyOD Publishing, Seattle, WA, 2015, including materials created by Dr. John Wallen, which are accessed through the public domain.)

DISCUSSION OF RESPONSES TO EXERCISE F-1

1. a. **No.** Commands such as these convey strong emotion, but do not name what feeling prompted the speaker.
   b. **D.** Speaker says he feels annoyed.
2. a. **No.** Questions that express strong feeling without naming it.
   b. **D.** Speaker says he feels resentment.
   c. **No.** Accusations that convey strong negative feelings. Because the feelings are not named, we do not know whether the accusations stemmed from anger, disappointment, hurt, or something else.
3. a. **D.** Speaker says he feels discouraged.
   b. **No.** The statement appears to describe what kind of day it was. In fact, it expresses the speaker's negative feelings without saying whether he feels depressed, annoyed, lonely, humiliated, rejected, or what.
4. a. **No.** This value judgment reveals positive feelings about the other person but does not describe what they are. Does the speaker like, respect, enjoy, admire, or love him/her?
   b. **D.** The speaker describes his positive feeling as respect.
5. a. **D.** A clear description of how the speaker feels when with the other person.
   b. **No.** First, the speaker does not speak for himself but hides behind the phrase, "we feel." Second, "you're a wonderful person" is a value judgment and not a feeling.
   c. **No.** The statement does name a feeling (likes) but the speaker attributes it to everybody and does not make clear that the feeling is within the speaker. A description of feeling must contain, "I," "me," "my," or "mine" to make clear that the feelings are the speaker's own or are within him/her. Does it seem more affectionate for a person to tell you, "I like you" or "everybody likes you"?
6. a. **No.** Conveys negative feelings by talking about the condition of things in this organization. Does not say what the speaker's inner state is.
   b. **No.** A question that expresses a negative value judgment about the organization. It does not describe what the speaker is feeling.
   c. **D.** A clear description of how the speaker feels in relation to his job. He feels afraid.

Expressions a and b are criticisms of the organization that could come from the kind of fear described in c. Negative criticisms and value judgments often sound like expressions of anger. In fact, negative value judgments and accusations often are the result of the speaker's fear, hurt feelings, disappointment, or loneliness.

7. a. **No.** A negative value judgment that conveys negative feelings, but does not say what kind they are.

   b. **No.** Although the speaker begins by saying, "I feel..." he/she does not name the feeling. Instead, he passes a negative value judgment on the exercise. Merely tacking the words "I feel" on the front of the statement does not make it a description of feeling. People often say "I feel" when they mean "I think" or "I believe," for example, "I feel the Yankees will win" or "I feel you don't like me."

Many people who say they are unaware of what they feel—or say they don't have any feelings about something—habitually state value judgments without recognizing that this is the way their positive or negative feelings are expressed. The speaker could have said she/he felt confused or frustrated or annoyed, etc. She/he then would have been describing her/his feelings without evaluating the exercise itself.

Many arguments could be avoided if we were careful to describe our feelings instead of expressing them through value judgments. For example, if Joe says the exercise is poor, and Fred says it is good, they may argue about which it "really" is. However, if Joe says he was frustrated by the exercise and Fred says he was interested and stimulated by it, no argument should follow. Each person's feelings are what they are. Of course, discussing what it means that each feels as he does may provide helpful information about each person and about the exercise itself.

8. a. **D.** Speaker says he feels inadequate.

   b. **No.** Careful! This sounds much the same as the previous statement. However, it states that the speaker actually IS inadequate—not that she/he just currently feels this way. The speaker has evaluated her/himself- has passed a negative judgement on her/himself—and has labeled her/himself as inadequate.

This subtle difference was introduced because many people confuse feeling and being. A person may feel inadequate to contribute to a group and yet make helpful contributions. Likewise, she/he may feel adequate and yet perform very inadequately. A person may feel hopeless about a situation that turns out not to be hopeless. One sign of emotional maturity is that a person does not confuse what she/he feels with the nature of the situation around him/her. Such a person knows she/he can perform adequately even though she/he feels inadequate to the task. She/he does not let her/his feelings keep her/him from doing her/his best because she/he knows the difference between feelings and performance and that the two do not always match.

9. a. **No.** The speaker has evaluated her/himself—passed a negative judgment—and labeled her/himself a failure.

   b. **No.** Instead of labeling her/himself a failure, the speaker blames the teacher. This is another value judgment and not a description of feelings.

   c. **D.** The speaker says she/he feels depressed.

   Statements a and c illustrate the important difference between passing judgments on oneself and describing one's feelings. Feelings can and do change. To say that I am depressed now does not imply that I will or must always feel the same. However, if I label myself as a failure—if I truly think of myself as a failure—I increase the probability that I will act like a failure.

   One woman stated this important insight for herself this way, "I have always thought I was a shy person. Many new things I really would have liked to do I avoided—I'd tell myself I was too shy. Now I have discovered that I am not shy, although at times I feel shy." Many of us avoid trying new things and thus learning, by labeling ourselves: "I'm not artistic," "I'm not creative," "I'm not articulate," "I can't speak in groups." If we could recognize what our feeling is beneath such statements, maybe we would be more willing to risk doing things we are somewhat fearful of.

10. a. **D.** The speaker says he feels lonely and isolated.

    b. **No.** Conveys negative feelings but does not say whether he/she feels lonely, angry, disappointed, hurt, or what.

    c. **No.** Instead of "I feel," the speaker should have said, "I believe." The last part of the statement really tells what the speaker believes the others feel about him/her not what he/she feels.

    Expressions c and a relate to each other as follows: "Because I believe that nobody in my group cares whether I am there or not, I feel lonely and isolated."

Good work! At this point, you should be more capable of distinguishing between thoughts and feelings, and more capable of clearly conveying your own emotions when you want to do so.

To borrow from the pioneering work of family systems therapists Murray Bowen and Edwin Friedman, you are becoming a more "self-differentiated" person. You are more clearly defining aspects of yourself—what you think, what you feel, and what you want—as distinct from what others think, feel, and want. This process of self-respect, of really paying attention to and understanding yourself, is essential to truly understanding and respecting others. Without self-differentiation, one is likely to be wrapped up in either a drama of catering to the real and imagined emotions and wants of others, or in an equally dramatic rebellion against the demands you perceive them to be imposing, or both, bouncing like a yo-yo between the two extremes of "being nice" and "standing up" for yourself. You are taking steps toward a calmer, more thoughtful path.

Let us continue. You have sharpened your ability to distinguish between your interpretations and the words, body language, and tone of voice that you are interpreting. Now continue your skill building with more of Mr. Wallen's wisdom. And keep this simple rule in mind during tense situations: "When in doubt, paraphrase."

PARAPHRASE

A Basic Communication Skill for Improving Interpersonal Relationships

by John Wallen

The problem: Tell somebody your phone number and he will usually repeat it to make sure he heard it correctly. However, if you make a complicated statement, most people will express agreement or disagreement, without trying to ensure that they are responding to what you intended. Most people seem to assume that what they understand from a statement is what the other intended.

How do you check to make sure that you understood another person's ideas or suggestions as he intended them? How do you know that his remark means the same to you as it does to him?

Of course, you can get the other person to clarify his remark by asking, "what do you mean?" or "tell me more" or by saying "I don't understand." However, after he has elaborated you still face the same question: "Am I understanding his idea as he intended it to be understood?" Your feeling of certainty is no evidence that you do, in fact, understand.

The skill: If you state, in your own way, what his remark conveys to you, the other can begin to determine whether his message is coming through as he intended. Then if he thinks you misunderstand, he can speak directly to the misunderstanding that you have revealed. I will use the term "paraphrase" *for any means of showing the other person what his idea or suggestion means to you.*

Paraphrasing, then, is a way of revealing your understanding of the other person's comment in order to test your understanding. An additional benefit of paraphrasing is that it lets others know that you are interested in them. It is evidence that you do want to understand what they mean.

If you can show the other person that you really do understand their point, they will probably be willing to attempt to understand your view.

Thus, paraphrasing is crucial in attempting to bridge the interpersonal gap:

1. It increases the accuracy of communication and, thus, the degree of mutual shared understanding.
2. The act of paraphrasing itself conveys feeling—your interest in the other, your concern to see how they view things.

Learning to paraphrase: People sometimes think of paraphrasing as merely putting the other persons' words in another way, then try to say the same thing with different words. Such word-swapping may merely result in the illusion of mutual understanding, as in the following example:

Sarah: Jim should never have become a teacher.
Fred: You mean teaching isn't the right job for him?
Sarah: Exactly! Teaching is not the right job for him.

Instead of trying to reword Sarah's statement, Fred might have asked himself, "What does Sarah's statement mean to me?" In that case, the interchange might have sounded like this:

Sarah: Jim should never have become a teacher.
Fred: You mean he is too harsh on the children? Maybe even cruel?

Sarah: Oh no. I meant that he has such expensive tastes that he can't ever earn enough as a teacher.

Fred: Oh, I see. You think he should have gone into a field that would have ensured him a higher standard of living.

Sarah: Exactly! Teaching is not the right job for Jim.

Effective paraphrasing is not a trick or a verbal gimmick. It comes from an attitude, a desire to know what the other means. And to satisfy this desire, you reveal the meaning his comment had for you so that the other can say whether it matched the meaning he intended to convey.

If the other's statement was general, it may convey something specific to you:

Larry: I think this is a very poor textbook.

You: Do you mean that it has too many inaccuracies?

Larry: No, the text is accurate, but the book comes apart too easily.

Possibly the other person's comment suggests an example to you:

Laura: This text had too many omissions; we shouldn't adopt it.

You: Do you mean, for example, that it contains nothing about the role of African Americans in the development of America?

Laura: Yes, that is one example. It also lacks a discussion of the development of the arts in America.

If the speaker's comment was very specific, it may convey a more general idea to you:

Ralph: Do you have 25 pencils I can borrow for my class?

You: Do you just want something for them to write with? I have 15 ballpoint pens and 10 or 11 pencils.

Ralph: Anything that will write will do.

Sometimes the other's ideas will suggest the inverse or opposite to you:

Stanley: I think the teacher's union acts too irresponsibly, because the administration has ignored them for so long.

You: Do you mean that the TU would be less militant now if the administration had consulted with them in the past?

Stanley: Certainly, I think the TU is being forced to more and more des-
perate measures.

To develop your skill in understanding others, try different ways of

1. Conveying your interest in understanding what they mean.
2. Revealing what the other's statement meant to you. Find out what
   kinds of responses are helpful ways of paraphrasing for you.

The next time someone is angry with you or is criticizing you, try to paraphrase until you can demonstrate that you understand what he or she is
trying to convey as they intend it. Be a scientist of your own interactions—
what effect does paraphrasing have on you and on the other person?

PERCEPTION CHECK

Wallen's fourth tool, "perception check," consists of naming your hunch
about what someone else is feeling. In other words, a perception check
is using feeling description to communicate your perception of someone
else's emotion. For example, depending on your judgment about how they
will take it and whether it will be useful, you might say, "you seem (sad,
mad, glad, afraid, or any variation thereof)."

To generate a perception check, you must pay attention to the other person's verbal and nonverbal sources of information (words, tone, body language, and facial expressions), and take into account their circumstances
(they just joined the company, they just lost a loved one, etc.). Then you
match the external data with what you have felt in similar circumstances, or
have felt when your verbal and nonverbal behavior was similar to that of the
other person. Drawing on these sources of internal and external information, a perception check is then one's best guess about the other's emotions.

This may sound complicated. Like many processes of perception, when
we break it down, it *is* complicated. It is also yet another constant and
lightning-quick process (like interpretation of meaning), usually occurring outside of conscious awareness. If you think about it, you will probably agree that you have hunches all the time about how others are feeling.
Wallen helps us bring the process into awareness. This helps in two
ways: we can get better and better at tuning in to others, and somewhat

paradoxically, we can be less attached to our beliefs about what others are feeling.

In practical terms, perception check can help close gaps by providing a way to convey empathy and by increasing your understanding of the other by helping you find out whether your hunch matches their own beliefs about how they are feeling.

Keep in mind that emotions are, well, emotional, and people deny them in themselves and try to control them in others ("Don't feel sad"). Communication about emotion can be tricky. If a person believes you are pointing out their emotions as if it's a fault, they may respond defensively. Nonetheless, a perception check can have the desired impact, especially if you are acting with genuine empathy, and you are conveying that successfully to the recipient. Paying attention to and respecting the emotions of people you care about is important if you want to truly connect. Paying attention to and respecting your own emotions is the surest way to hone your ability to empathize with others.

That brings us near the end of my chapter on Wallen's four skills. As I trust you can see, Wallen's interpersonal gap is potentially much more than just a theory. As corny as this may sound, *it is a way of (interpersonal) life*. Given that potential, further exploration is called for. My colleague and brother Chris wrote the following article to assist such exploration.

But first, let me say a little about "self-generation" (a concept Chris is about to introduce to you). Self-generation is what is coming from inside of you that you are accessing in interpersonal interactions. Sometimes this is current data, such as your feelings. Especially in reactive moments, it is past experiences that you are projecting onto others in the present. As mentioned, authority figures are like blank screens for "projection." They remind us emotionally of the authority figures in our early lives, and it takes awareness to see them in the present as the people they really are. To the extent possible, it is important to be able to differentiate between and to be aware of what is truly current, and what is coming from the past. Try to remember that negative interpretations of others are more about past experiences (your hippocampus is doing its job of carrying emotional memories) than they are about the person you are presently interacting with. That awareness will help you not get too attached to those interpretations, and that is vital for closing gaps and keeping your brain in open learner mode. Chris will explore this distinction between what is inside of you and what is truly outside while also giving you some practical tips on how to use Wallen's behavioral skills to close gaps. Following that, you'll be well equipped for application, practice, and learning from experience!

Appendix B: Crosby Leadership Quiz

Answer each question below using the following scale.

A (almost always), F (frequently), O (occasionally), S (seldom), N (almost never)

1. _____ Goals are clear, achievable, measurable (through simple metrics) and aligned (safety and production goals don't clash, for example).

2. _____ I ensure all employees understand their goals and have metrics to evaluate their work.

3. _____ I oversee a manageable number of initiatives that, more often than not, yield the desired results.

4. _____ I effectively hold people accountable, and ensure the same in the layers below.

5. _____ When I identify business critical performance issues, I drive effective problem-solving activities until a solution is in place that is achieving consistent results.

6. _____ Individuals are assigned single point accountability (SPA) for all tasks, decisions, and projects, and anyone they will impact/depend on are informed.

7. _____ I ensure clarity about who will do what and by when in every situation requiring action at my level and below.

8. _____ I effectively monitor critical issues and actions, and intervene when items are slipping.

9. _____ I communicate which decisions I am making, who can influence me, how, and by when.

10. _____ Who decides what is based on business results (i.e., who decides to expedite an order; who decides to stop production to prevent scrap, etc.).

11. _____ I regularly assess (with input) whether meetings and reports are meeting their intended purpose, and whether their value outweighs the time and effort they consume in the layers below me.

12. _____ I ensure that individuals, groups, and departments are giving and getting what they need from each other.

13. _____ I ensure effective resolutions when conflict between any parties (whether individuals, groups, locations, etc.) is interfering with business results.

14. _____ I interact with all layers and groups that impact my area's performance, staying current and connected (while being mindful not to skip layers when giving direction).

15. _____ End-users are engaged in an effective manner prior to making changes that will impact their work.

16. _____ I hold the same standard of behavior when managing my interactions with my peers and superiors as I want my subordinates to hold with me (surfacing issues, etc.).

17. _____ I make sure I understand the message, and I don't shoot the messenger even if the delivery is unpolished or the message is hard for me to hear.

18. _____ I take clear positions on work issues. I accomplish balance in most interactions, neither doing most of the talking, nor leaving people guessing about where I stand.

19. _____ I give timely and behaviorally specific feedback (free of judgment words, such as "unprofessional"), both positive and negative, and ensure the same in the layers below me.

20. _____ I am a calming influence when others are reactive.

21. _____ I work conflicts when they are small, rather than letting them build into larger issues, and ensure the same in the layers below me.

22. _____ I pay attention to the emotions of others, and effectively convey understanding of their situation.

23. _____ I paraphrase to verify whether I understood, especially if I am troubled by what I am hearing.

24. _____ I ensure the entire workforce is engaged in surfacing and solving work issues.

25. _____ I am neither under- nor over-managing.

© Crosby & Associates

CROSBY & ASSOCIATES WEIGHTED SCORING ANSWER SHEET:

How to score: Use the weighted scoring answer sheet (Table B.1) and mark the corresponding number for each question. Then total each column to get your final score.

Why the weights? Based on the Likert scale, we do not think the categories of occasionally, seldom, or almost never deserve many, if any, points. The above scale represents our best judgment of what we think creates an exceptional leader on the dimensions given.

What do the scores mean? We think if you score at or above 100 you are an exceptional leader. Scoring 50 to 100 means you do many things quite well, and below 50 means you have some work to do on these leadership dimensions.

TABLE B.1

Crosby Leadership Quiz Weighted Scoring Sheet (Created by the Author)

	Almost Always	Frequently	Occasionally	Seldom	Almost Never
1	5	1			
2	5	3			
3	5	3	1		
4	5	3			
5	5	1			
6	5	3			
7	5	2			
8	5	1			
9	5	4	1		
10	5	2			
11	2	5	1		
12	5	3	1		
13	5	3			
14	5	3			
15	5	2			
16	5	4	1		
17	5	4			
18	5	3			
19	5	3			
20	5	1			
21	5	2			
22	5	3			
23	5	4	1		
24	5	3			
25	5	3			
Totals					
Total of all columns - Final Score→					

Bibliography

Amen, D. (1998). *Change Your Brain, Change Your Life.* New York: Three Rivers Press.

Collins, J. (2001). *Good to Great.* New York: HarperCollins.

Covey, S. (1989). *The Seven Habits of Highly Effective People.* New York: Simon & Schuster.

Crosby, C. (2016). *Strategic Organizational Alignment: Authority, Power, Results.* New York: Business Expert Press.

Crosby, G. (2015). *Fight, Flight, Freeze: Emotional Intelligence, Behavioral Science, Systems Theory & Leadership* (Third Edition). Seattle, WA: CrosbyOD Publishing.

Crosby, R.P. (1992). *Walking the Empowerment Tightrope.* King of Prussia, PA: Organization Design and Development, Inc.

Crosby, R.P. (1995). *Organizational Structural Change: A Trap or a Path?*

Crosby, R.P. (2011). *Culture Change in Organizations.* Seattle, WA: CrosbyOD Publishing.

Crosby, R.P. (2015). *The Cross-Functional Workplace.* Seattle, WA: CrosbyOD Publishing.

Dyer, W. (1998). *Wisdom of the Ages.* New York: HarperCollins.

Fair, C. (1971). *From the Jaws of Victory.* New York: Simon & Schuster.

Frankl, V. (1963). *Man's Search for Meaning.* New York: Simon & Schuster.

Friedman, E. (1985). *Generation to Generation.* New York: Guilford Press.

Friedman, E. (1991). "Bowen Theory and Therapy," in *Handbook of Family Therapy, Volume II,* edited by Gurman and Kniskern.

Friedman, E. (2007). *A Failure of Nerve.* New York, NY: Church Publishing.

GAO-08-1051T—United States Government Accountability Office testimony—Jul 2008 (OMB and agencies need to improve planning, management and oversight of projects).

Garrett, R. (1976). *Clash of Arms: The World's Great Land Battles.* New York: Galahad Books.

Gazzaniga, M. (2011). *Who's in Charge?* New York: HarperCollins Publishers.

Gold, M. (Editor). (1999). *The complete Social Scientist: A Kurt Lewin Reader.* Washington, DC. The American Psychological Association.

Goleman, D. (2003). *Destructive Emotions.* New York: Bantam Dell.

Goleman, D., Boyatzis, R., McKee, A. (2002). *Primal Leadership.* Boston: Harvard Business School Publishing.

Hall, J. (1969). *Conflict Management Survey.* Teleometrics International Inc.

Hanson, V. (1999). *The Soul of Battle.* New York: Anchor Books.

Herman, A. (2008). *Gandhi & Churchill.* New York: Bantom Dell.

IT Week Magazine, 19 May 2008.

Johnson, J. (1975). *Doing Field Research.* New York: The Free Press.

Kerr, M. and Bowen, M. (1988). *Family Evaluation.* New York: W.W. Norton & Co.

Lewin, K. (1951). *Field Theory in Social Science: Selected Theoretical Papers* (D. Cartwright, Ed.). New York: Harper & Row.

Lewin, K. (1997). *Resolving Social Conflicts & Field Theory in Social Science.* Washington, DC: American Psychological Association.

Lewis, T., Amini, A. and Lannon, R. (2000). *A General Theory of Love.* New York: Random House.

Mehrabian, A. (1981). *Silent Messages.* Belmont, CA: Wadsworth.

Merton, T. (2004). *A Year with Thomas Merton*. San Francisco: Harper.

Minuchin, S. (1974). *Families and Family Therapy*. Boston: Harvard University Press.

Rogers, C. (1961). *On Becoming a Person*. New York: Houghton Mifflin.

Ruiz, D.M. (1997). *The Four Agreements*. San Rafael, CA: Amber Allen Publishing.

Santayana, G. (1905). *The Life of Reason: Reason in Common Sense*. Scribner's.

Satir, V. (1972). *People Making*. Palo Alto, CA: Science and Behavior Books.

Senge, P. (1990). *The Fifth Discipline*. New York: Double Day/Currency.

Siegel, D. (1999). *The Developing Mind*. New York. Guildford Press.

Siegel, D. (2010). *Mindsight*. New York: Bantam Books.

Thurman, H. (2006). *Howard Thurman; Essential Writings*. Maryknoll, NY: Orbis Books.

Tolle, E. (1999). *The Power of Now*. Novato, CA: New World Library.

Wallen, J. *The Interpersonal Gap*. Unpublished.

Williamson, D. (1991). *The Intimacy Paradox*. New York: Guildford Press.

Index